CONVERSATIONS WITH...
SIR ARTHUR CONAN DOYLE

CONVERSATIONS WITH...
SIR ARTHUR CONAN DOYLE

SIMON PARKE

Conversations with… Sir Arthur Conan Doyle

White Crow Books is an imprint of
White Crow Productions Ltd
PO Box 1013
Guildford GU1 9EJ

www.whitecrowbooks.com

Text design and eBook production by Essential Works
www.essentialworks.co.uk

ISBN 978-1-907355-80-6
eBook ISBN 978-1-907355-82-0
Audiobook ISBN 978-1-907355-81-3

Religion & Spirituality

Distributed in the UK by
Lightning Source Ltd.
Chapter House
Pitfield
Kiln Farm
Milton Keynes MK11 3LW

Distributed in the USA by
Lightning Source Inc.
246 Heil Quaker Boulevard
LaVergne
Tennessee 37086

Contents

Preface

The conversation presented here is imagined; but Doyle's words are not. All of Sir Arthur's words included here are his own, taken from his extensive writings and correspondence.

The only alteration to his original words has been the occasional addition of a link word to help the flow.

But such small and rare additions never alter either his mood or meaning. After all, to discover the man and his meaning is the reason for this adventure; so these are his passions, and his words, with one exception. He didn't say 'Elementary, my dear Simon!'

Though it would not have been out of character....

Introduction

These interviews were conducted over a period of three days, after Sir Arthur kindly agreed to reflect with me on his energetic and varied life.

We meet at Windlesham, his house in Crowborough, Sussex; some way from his Edinburgh birth place. We talk mainly in his bedroom, to which his angina now confines him. But sometimes we're in the garden, where his love of the outdoor life is clear to see. His spirit still adventures, even if his body groans. At 71 years of age, he remains a big man, with a kindly face, which one publisher likened to that of a walrus. I can see what he meant.

In many ways, Sir Arthur Conan Doyle is a Boy's Own figure, full of derring-do. He has written historical novels; short stories of horror and the supernatural; been a fine cricketer (he once took the wicket of the great W. G. Grace) and played football, rugby and golf. He has campaigned for underdogs like George Edalji and the victims of brutal conditions in the Congo Free State; introduced skis to Switzerland and had the strange idea of a channel tunnel linking England and France. He has known friendship with both Harry Houdini and Oscar Wilde; had breakfast with Lloyd George; been a ship's doctor in the arctic, a war reporter in South Africa and is a popular knight of the realm. He has toured the USA, Canada, Australia, South Africa and Europe. Most notably of all, he created Sherlock Holmes – perhaps the world's most famous detective.

Yet as we meet, Sir Arthur is a man under siege because for the last quarter of his life, alongside the above, he has become the world's most famous proponent of spiritualism; also known as 'contacting the dead.' It has bought ridicule from literary, scientific and religious figures; and been an embarrassment for many who preferred Holmes' dry humanist logic, to such apparent gullibility.

Only last January, the writer H. G. Wells launched a savage

attack on Doyle in the *Sunday Express*, in response to his book *Pheneas Speaks*. In this book, Doyle published the recorded messages of a spirit-figure called Pheneas, as expressed through the mediumship of his second wife, Jean. In the introduction, Doyle had written: 'We would beg the most orthodox reader to bear in mind that God is still in touch with mankind; and that there is as much reason that he should send messages and instructions to a suffering and distracted world as ever there was in days of old.'

I have with me the press cuttings of Wells' response. He calls Pheneas 'a platitudinous bore' who had been promising wonderful changes for the world since 1922, but with no apparent fulfilment. He writes: 'This Pheneas, I venture to think, is an imposter wrought of self-deception; as pathetic as a rag doll which some lonely child has made for its own comfort. We are told of floods of spiritual light! Wonderful prophecies are spoken of – but where are they?'

The row over Pheneas has been typical of the disputes that have surrounded Doyle in recent years; disputes which have left him an isolated figure. Not that he bends with the wind in any way at all, for Doyle is a stubborn man. When he was but twenty, on his first night on board an arctic whaler, he knocked down the ship's steward in a boxing match; and 50 years on, he is still up for the fight.

Who would have thought that the creator of Sherlock Holmes would end his days in this way? Hero or embarrassment? Visionary or lunatic? There is so much to talk about, as I sit down for conversations with... Sir Arthur Conan Doyle.

ONE

A man under fire

SP: I suppose like many people, Sir Arthur, I'm wondering why the creator of Sherlock Holmes threw it all away to become an evangelist for the spiritualist movement, which to be honest, has a slightly dubious reputation.

ACD: People call me credulous but they don't know what the evidence is. I say any man who had the evidence I had, and didn't believe it, would be a lunatic.

SP: But you have become like a missionary for this cause. Is it worth it?

ACD: This movement, so long the subject of sneers and ridicule, is absolutely the most important development in the whole history of the human race.

SP: Really? That's some claim.

ACD: So important that, if we could conceive one single man discovering and publishing it, he would rank before Christopher Columbus as a discoverer of new worlds, before Paul as a teacher of new religious truths, and before Isaac Newton as a student of the laws of the Universe

SP: So this is a new type of knowledge?

ACD: Psychic science, though still in its infancy, has already reached a point where we can dissect many of those occurrences which were regarded as inexplicable in past ages; and can classify and even explain them – so far as any ultimate explanation of anything is possible.

SP: You call it a science. But what has it achieved in that domain?

ACD: So long as gravity, electricity, magnetism and so many other great natural forces are inexplicable one must not ask too much of the youngest – though it is also the oldest – of the sciences. But the progress made has been surprising; and the more surprising since it has been done by a limited circle of students whose results have hardly reached the world at large, and have been greeted with incredulous contempt rather than with the appreciation they deserve.

SP: But doesn't this take us back to the dubious reputation of the movement; dubious because of the many instances when mediums have been revealed as cheats and charlatans?

ACD: As to the personality of mediums, they have seemed to me to be very average specimens of the community, neither markedly better nor markedly worse.

But spiritualism is no more to be judged by venal public mediums than Christianity is to be condemned because in every church there are a certain number of hypocrites and time-servers.

SP: Fair point.

ACD: Yes, the movement has been disfigured by many grievous incidents, which may explain – but does not excuse – the perverse opposition which it encounters in so many quarters.

SP: So tell me: beyond the fakes and frauds, why are the attacks on you so savage? What exactly is being threatened?

ACD: This opposition is largely based upon the absolute

materialism of the age, which will not admit that there can exist at the present moment, such conditions as might be accepted in the far past. When these religious people are actually brought in contact with that life beyond the grave which they profess to believe in – they wince, recoil and declare it impossible!

SP: That does seem odd.

ACD: And the science of the day is also rooted in materialism, and discards all its own very excellent axioms when it is faced by an entirely new and unexpected proposition. Faraday, for instance, declared that in approaching a new subject one should make up one's mind a priori as to what is possible and what is not!

SP: Hardly an open mind, I can see.

ACD: While Huxley said that the messages, even if true, 'interested him no more than the gossip of curates in a cathedral city.'

SP: Nice turn of phrase. And even Darwin chipped in, didn't he?

ACD: Darwin said: 'God help us if we are to believe such things.'

SP: But without wishing to labour the point, Sir Arthur, it is well known that a number of mediums are alcoholics.

ACD: A temptation to which several great mediums have succumbed is that of drink, yes. This comes about in a very natural way, for overworking the power leaves them in a state of physical prostration, and the stimulus of alcohol affords a welcome relief, and may tend at last to become a custom and finally a curse. Alcoholism always weakens the moral sense, so that these degenerate mediums yield themselves more readily to fraud, with the result that several who had deservedly won honoured names and met all hostile criticism have, in their later years, been detected in the most contemptible tricks. It is a thousand pities that it should be so, but if the Court of Arches were to give up its secrets –

SP: – that's the highest court in the Church of England –

ACD: – it would be found that tippling and moral degeneration were by no means confined to psychics.

SP: Well that's a fact. It's just that mediums – in bringing dead loved ones back to life – are claiming a most important role for themselves; and so trust in them is crucial.

ACD: A medium is in no sense a teacher or an example, but is a passive instrument for forces outside her self. There have been, and are, many mediums who have been of saintly mould. There have been others who have yielded to some human weakness, very especially to drink. Their powers and their message are to be held distinct from themselves, as a Catholic would hold that a bad priest might celebrate a true sacrament; or a materialist that a foolish operator may transmit a wise telegram. Their weaknesses delay the acceptance of the new knowledge. It still stands upon the threshold – but the door is slowly opening.

SP: I know you are not happy with mediums being paid by results.

ACD: The whole system of paying by results – which is practically the present system, since if a medium never gets results he would soon get no payments – is a vicious one. It is only when the professional medium can be guaranteed an annuity which will be independent of results, that we can eliminate the strong temptation to substitute pretended phenomena, when the real ones are wanting.

SP: What other lessons have been learned?

ACD: We have learned that there are many forms of mediumship, so different from each other that an expert at one may have no powers at all at the other. The automatic writer, the clairvoyant, the crystal-seer, the trance speaker, the photographic medium, the direct voice medium and others, are all, when genuine, the manifestations of one force, which runs through varied channels as it did in the gifts ascribed to the disciples.

SP: The whole 'darkness' thing is an issue as well. Mediums always want the séance to take place in the dark, which does raise suspicions that there's something to hide.

ACD: The unhappy outburst of roguery was helped, no doubt, by the need for darkness claimed by the early experimenters – a claim which is by no means essential, since the greatest of all mediums, D. D. Home, was able by the exceptional strength of his powers, to dispense with it. At the same time, the fact that darkness rather than light, and dryness rather than moisture, are helpful to good results has been abundantly manifested, and points to the physical laws which underlie the phenomena.

SP: Some think it's just all a bit weird. Dark rooms; hysterical clients; calling the dead; strange apparitions. Can this really be healthy for those involved?

ACD: There is much force in the criticism that too constant intercourse with the affairs of another world may distract our attention and weaken our powers in dealing with our obvious duties in this one. A séance, with the object of satisfying curiosity or of rousing interest, cannot be an elevating influence; and the mere sensation-monger can make this holy and wonderful thing as base as the over-indulgence in a stimulant.

s p: But the other side of the coin is that you don't believe the sceptics have looked at it properly?

a c d: My experiences with mediums, good, bad and indifferent, are probably as wide as those of any living man. With so much practical work behind me, the reader can imagine my feelings when in a public debate upon the subject with Dr. Haldane of Cambridge my distinguished opponent said, 'I once knew a medium.' In my reply I asked him what he would think of me if I contradicted him upon some point of chemistry, and said, 'I have once been in a laboratory.'

s p: Some people see providence in this; mysterious and miraculous events of a divine nature. Is this how you see it, Sir Arthur?

a c d: The phrase may well represent a fact, but people must learn that no such thing has ever been known as an interposition of providence, save through natural law; and that when it has seemed inexplicable and miraculous, it is only because the law has not yet been understood. All miracles come under exact law; but the law, like all natural laws, is itself divine and miraculous.

s p: So the message is: whatever the cost, and whatever the ridicule, you will carry on saying what you're saying?

a c d: There are certain things which it is my duty to say, and this seems to be the time to do it. They are not easy things, nor things which make for popularity; but for many years I have had to plead an unpopular cause for the sake of truth, and one gets used to opposition and misrepresentation.

TWO

From such beginnings

It is not something that Sir Arthur ever talks about, but his father, Charles Doyle, was an alcoholic. And it was the young Arthur himself who co-signed the committal papers necessary to have him placed in a lunatic asylum.

Charles Doyle was clearly a sensitive individual from the outset of his career. He began drinking early in life, but the habit intensified after marriage. It was not long before he could no longer support or cope with his family. There was family embarrassment as he spent his final years, from 1885 to 1893, in three asylums. This followed time spent in a nursing home which specialized in the care of alcoholics, after he had become drunkenly violent at home.

Sir Arthur's mother Mary was of Irish origin and proudly traced her family back to Percys of Northumberland, and from there to the Plantagenet line. So his childhood love for 15th-century tales of noble chivalry is perhaps unsurprising. Fed by their mother's story telling, here was a family who, in the face of shame and relative poverty, clung tight to past glories.

SP: Your childhood was not the easiest.

ACD: Perhaps it was good for me that times were hard, for I was wild, full-bloodied and a trifle reckless. But the situation called for energy and application, so that one was bound to try and meet it. My mother had been so splendid that I could not fail her.

SP: Your mother was an important figure for you; you wrote regularly to her throughout her life. What was so good about her?

ACD: In my early childhood, as far as I can remember anything at all, the vivid stories she would tell me stand out so clearly that they obscure the real facts of my life.

SP: And your father?

ACD: He had a charm of manner and courtesy of bearing which I have seldom seen equalled. His wit was quick and playful. He possessed also a remarkable delicacy of mind which would give him moral courage enough to rise and leave any company which talked in a manner which was course. He was unworldly and unpractical and his family suffered for it; but even his faults were in some ways the result of his developed spirituality. He lived and died a fervent son of the Roman Catholic faith.

SP: A few years ago, you mounted an exhibition of your father's painting?

ACD: Indeed. And the critics were surprised to find what a great and original artist he was – by far the greatest, in my opinion, of the family. His brush was concerned with fairies and delicate themes of the kind; but with wild and fearsome subjects, so that his work had a very particular style of its own, mitigated by great natural humour.

SP: Clearly he had a vivid imagination. As one critic said, 'His mind soared and dipped among giant animals, strange sprites, confrontations of the grotesque and mundane.'

ACD: He was more terrible than Blake and less morbid than Wiertz!

SP: And your home in Edinburgh? You say it was not in the best or most peaceful part of town.

ACD: We lived in a cul de sac street, with a very vivid life of its own and a fierce feud between the small boys on either side of it. Finally, it was fought out between two champions, I representing the poorer boys who lived in the flats, and my opponent, the richer boys who lived in the opposite villas. We fought in the garden of one of the said villas, and had an excellent contest of many rounds, not being strong enough to weaken each other.

SP: So you hit each other; but not to any great effect. And then when you were nine, you were sent away to a Jesuit preparatory school for two years.

ACD: The year was not broken up by the frequent holidays which illuminate the present educational period. Save for six weeks each summer, one never left the school.

SP: How did that feel?

ACD: On the whole, they were happy years. I could hold my own in both brain and strength with my comrades. I was fortunate enough to get under the care of a kindly principal, one Father Cassidy, who was more human then Jesuits normally are. I have always kept a warm remembrance of this man, and of his gentle ways to the little boys – young rascals many of us – who were committed to his care.

SP: And were you a writer then?

ACD: Oh yes. On a wet half-holiday, I would be elevated on a desk and with an audience of little boys squatting on the floor, with their chins upon their hands, I would talk myself husky over the misfortunes of my heroes!

SP: You had characters in your head even then?

ACD: Week in and week out those unhappy men have battled and striven and groaned for the amusement of that little circle.

SP: And was this out of the kindness of your heart – or was there perhaps some reward for your stories?

ACD: I was bribed with pastry to continue these efforts, and I remember I always stipulated tarts. Oh yes, it was strict business, which shows that I was born to be a member of the Authors' Society!

SP: But then the transition to the Jesuit Public school at Stoneyhurst.

ACD: Corporal punishment was severe, and I think I can speak with feelings as I think few, if any boys of my time, endured more of it.

SP: Why was that? Were you especially naughty?

ACD: I was more beaten than others not because I was in anyway vicious, but it was that I had a nature which responded eagerly to affectionate kindness, which I never received; but which in turn rebelled against threats and took a perverted pride in showing that it would not be cowed by violence.

SP: And ironically, it was here, in this bastion of Christian faith, that you began to leave it, never to return. When did the rot set in?

ACD: I heard Father Murphy, a fierce Irish priest, declare that there was sure damnation for everyone outside the church. I looked upon him with horror, and to that moment I trace the first rift which has grown into a chasm between me and those who were my guides. We spiritualists, who by actual personal contact know something of the real conditions of the next life, are aware that this vision of flame and torture is a horrible chimera. It does not exist.

s p: And then you began your medical studies in 1876. Looking back, what have you to say about Scottish universities?

a c d: The young aspirant pays his pound, and finds himself a student.

s p: And then the hard work begins?

a c d: No. After that, he may do absolutely what he will.

s p: Oh?

a c d: There are certain classes going on at certain hours, which he may attend if he choose. If not, he may stay away without the slightest remonstrance of his college. As to religion, he may worship the sun, or have a private fetish of his own upon the mantelpiece of his lodgings, for all the university cares!

s p: Exams?

a c d: Examinations are periodically held, at which he may appear or not, as he chooses. The university is a great unsympathetic machine, taking in a stream of raw-boned cartilaginous youths at one end, and turning them out at the other as learned divines, astute lawyers and skilful medical men. Of every thousand of the raw material, about six hundred emerge at the other side.

s p: And the remainder?

a c d: The remainder are broken in the process.

SP: And did you find yourself able to make friends with the lecturers? Presumably they became father-figures to some?

ACD: There was no attempt at friendship, or even acquaintance, between professors and students at Edinburgh. It was a strictly business arrangement by which you paid, for example, 4 guineas for Anatomy lectures and received the winter course in exchange; never seeing your professor save behind his desk and never under any circumstance exchanging words with him. They were remarkable men, however, some of these professors; and we managed to know them pretty well without any personal acquaintance.

SP: And of course one of them – Doctor Joseph Bell – went on to become particularly well known – as the model for Sherlock Holmes, who I wish to focus on in our next conversation. But it seems fitting, Sir Arthur, as we close this conversation about your youth, to mention your trip to the Arctic in the whaling boat *Hope* – on which, at the age of 20, you were offered the post of Ship's Surgeon.

ACD: I went on board the whaler a big struggling youth. I came off a powerful well-grown man.

SP: And it was a long hard voyage, was it not, with a crew of fifty?

ACD: Indeed.

SP: Strong gales and pack ice – but looking back across the years, what do you most remember?

ACD: The perpetual light, the glare of the white ice, the deep blue of the water, these are things which one remembers most clearly; and the dry, crisp, exhilarating air, which makes mere life the keenest of pleasures.

SP: It seems the arctic had awakened the soul of a man born to wander.

THREE

Elementary, my dear Watson

Sherlock Holmes plunged to his death, along with his arch-rival Moriarty, down a waterfall in the Alps. Doyle killed him off believing the character held him back from more important things, like his historical novels. Predictably, there was a huge public outcry, and in the face of large financial offers, Sherlock Holmes was in time resurrected for two more stories. The premise which allowed this about-turn was that Sherlock had faked his death and gone into temporary hiding, in order to avoid other dangerous enemies he'd made.

But if that was his end of the great detective, what was his beginning?

SP: So it is true that the great detective was based on a University lecturer of yours?

ACD: Joseph Bell was a thin wiry dark man, with a high-nosed acute face, penetrating grey eyes, angular shoulders. He would sit in his receiving room, with a face like a red Indian, and diagnose the people as they came in, before they ever opened their mouths.

SP: Those are some of my favourite bits in the books: when Holmes baffles Watson with his initial deductions, based solely on appearance.

ACD: Bell would tell people not only of their disease, but details of their past life; their occupation and place of residence; and hardly would he ever make a mistake.

SP: And in him, you found a man who combined scientific beliefs with humanistic beliefs, which attracted you. In his hands, science was not something mechanical, mere cause and effect; but something more fragile, more subtle and certainly influenced by psychological factors. Holmes exactly!

ACD: Dr Bell certainly had the most remarkable powers of observation, and I thought I'd try my hand at writing in which the detective treated crime, as Dr Bell treated a disease; and where science would take the place of chance.

SP: So you had the character. What about the stories?

ACD: Well, I thought of a hundred little dodges as you may say; a hundred little touches, by which he could build up his conclusions, and then I began to write stories on those lines. The result was Sherlock Holmes and I confess the result has surprised me very much!

SP: He was quickly everyone's favourite literary detective.

ACD: And to many, he seems to be a real person! I've had numerous letters addressed to him from all parts of the world, including an offer of marriage, and those who wish to be his house keeper.

SP: And you say that some countries like France, Egypt and China have actually founded their crime detection system on that of Holmes! Yet at the outset, when you were making a living as a doctor in Southsea, you never even considered yourself a writer – until, interestingly, a friend paid you a compliment.

ACD: Anyone observing my actions and tastes would have said that so strong a spring would certainly overflow. But for my own part, I never dreamed that I could produce decent prose, and the remark of my friend, who was by no means given to flattery, took me greatly by surprise.

SP: The power of encouragement.

ACD: So I sat down and wrote a little adventure story, which I call *The Mystery of Sasassa Valley*. To my great joy and surprise, it was accepted by *Chambers Journal* and I receive three guineas.

SP: And I'm told that the decision to write full time came to you when you were ill with influenza. Was that really the moment you finally gave up trying to combine a medical and a writing career?

ACD: Yes, it was a wild rush of joy. I remember in my delight taking the handkerchief which lay upon the coverlet in my enfeebled hand, and tossing it up to the ceiling in my exaltation. I should at last be my own master!

SP: Well, Sherlock Holmes certainly enabled you to be that. By 1920, you were one of the highest paid authors in the world. And one of the things that most interests me in the Sherlock Holmes stories is that the criminals often turn out to have their own reasons. There seems to be a rebellion in you against traditional ideas of sin.

ACD: When we view sin in the light of modern science, with the tenderness of the modern conscience, and with a sense of justice and proportion, it ceases to be that monstrous cloud which darkened the whole vision of the medieval theologian. Man has been more harsh with himself than an all-merciful God will ever be.

SP: Well, we'll get onto God. But even whilst writing the Holmes stories, your own passions – particularly your rage at established religion – were becoming apparent. In *The Sign of Four*, for instance, Holmes recommends to Watson a book by Reade, with the comment that 'It is one of the most remarkable books ever penned.' You remember?

ACD: I remember.

SP: Well, it may have been one of the most remarkable – but it was also one of the most controversial, Sir Arthur, and reckoned 'blasphemous' and 'obscene' by critics. You will recall its message?

ACD: Supernatural Christianity is false.

SP: That was the message of the book.

ACD: God-worship is idolatry. Prayer is useless. The soul is not immortal. There are no rewards and there are no punishments in a future state.

SP: Not quite your position now, perhaps.

ACD: Prior to 1886, I remained a sceptic about the after life.

SP: So what did you think about death in those days?

ACD: When the candle burns out, the light disappears. When the electric cell is shattered, the current stops. When the body dissolves, there is an end to the matter.

SP: So talk of any after-life was nonsense to you. You thought it was nothing more than a delusion; the self-important ego feeling it somehow should carry on.

ACD: It seemed to be a delusion, yes, and I was convinced that death did indeed end all.

SP: And there is also evidence of this scepticism in another of your stories, *The Ghosts of Goresthorpe Grange*, in which, ironically, you have some fun at spiritualism's expense!

ACD: Mea culpa.

SP: In the story, a man called D'odd is keen to find an occult presence in his new and spooky home. But disappointingly, he finds nothing spooky at all, and so advertises for a medium – only to hire one who turns out to be a fraud specializing in burglary. So D'odd then visits his friend, who has a list of possible mediums who might help. Perhaps, Sir Arthur, you could read the passage which describes their conversation in which they thumb through a directory in search of a medium:

ACD: 'What were you looking up again?'
  'Ghosts,' I suggested.
  'Of course, page 41. Here we are: 'J. H. Fowler and Son, Dunkel Street, suppliers of mediums to the nobility and gentry; charms sold, love philtres – mummies – horoscopes cast.' Nothing in your line there, I suppose?'
  I shook my head despondently.
  'Frederick Tabb,' he continued. 'Sole channel of communication between the living and the dead. Proprietor of the spirits of Byron, Kirke, White, Grimaldi, Tom Cribb and Inigo Jones. That's about the figure!'
  'Nothing romantic enough there,' I objected.
  'Here is another,' said my companion. 'Christopher McCarthy, bi-weekly séances – attended by all the eminent spirits of ancient and modern times. Nativities – charms – abracadabras, messages from the dead. He might be able to help us…'

SP: It's gracious of you to read something you wouldn't write now. But it's clear that you were indeed a sceptic in those days, and so was Sherlock Holmes. Yet getting back to the detective, in 1893, despite his massive popularity, you decide to kill him. Holmes meets his arch-enemy Moriarty in Switzerland, and disappears. Watson finds a letter from Holmes. Can you read for us the scene?

ACD: Watson read his dear friend's words: 'I have already explained to you, that my career had in any case reached its crisis, and that no possible conclusion to it could be more congenial to me than this.'

SP: And that was that; Sherlock Holmes exited stage left. A big step; but one you'd been planning a while. In 1891, you'd written to your mother of your intentions. What did you say?

ACD: I said, 'I think of slaying Holmes and winding him up for good and all. He takes my mind from better things.'

SP: And how did she reply?

ACD: 'You may do what you deem fit, Arthur, but the crowds will not take this light heartedly.'

SP: And they didn't, did they? With the death of Sherlock Holmes, fans wore mourning bands in the streets. You resurrected him in 1902, of course, with *The Hound of the Baskervilles*, and 1903, with *The Empty House* – but that then really was that; no more returns for the great man.

ACD: As I say, he took my mind from better things.

SP: In fact, you disowned him. You later wrote a stage play for Sherlock Holmes; and though little was left of your original script by the end of rehearsals, you didn't seem to mind! The play was panned by the critics; popular with the public, but it was your reply to the actor playing Holmes which most struck me. He asked permission to change Holmes' persona a little. To which you replied:

ACD: 'You may marry him, murder him or do anything you like to him!'

SP: He'd made you rich. But you really had said goodbye to Sherlock Holmes, hadn't you?

FOUR

The case of the lost religion

I have before me Ruth Brandon's description of Sir Arthur Conan Doyle. 'Sir Arthur,' she says, 'has many striking characteristics. He is gigantically tall and strong. He is a gifted story-teller. He is a man of strong opinions and considerable political influence. But perhaps the most extraordinary thing about him is the combination of all the attributes of worldly success with an almost child-like literalness and credulity of mind, manifested particularly in relation to spiritualism and its surrounding phenomena.'

In these later years, it has been spiritualism and not Sherlock that Doyle is famous for. He was educated in a strict Catholic school, and Jesuits are inclined to believe that if they have a child until the age of seven, then they have them for life. But this has not been true with Sir Arthur, whose life has become 'The case of the lost religion'.

ACD: Men have largely ceased to go to church. It is not that they are irreligious. It is that they have outgrown this presentiment of religion.

SP: You have already spoken a little of your disillusionment with established religion. You didn't warm to the savage God of some of your Jesuit teachers.

ACD: Were there ever any conscious blasphemers upon earth who have insulted the Deity so deeply as those extremists, be they Calvinist, Roman Catholic, Anglican or Jew, who pictured with their distorted minds an implacable torturer as the Ruler of the Universe!

SP: No established religion appealed to you after that.

ACD: Mankind must learn once for all that Religion has nothing whatever to do with theological beliefs or forms or ceremonies or priest hoods or vestments or sacraments or any of the other trappings and adornments which have so covered it, that we can no longer see it. It depends upon two things only, and those are Conduct and Character. If you are unselfish and kind then you are of the elect, call yourself what you will! If you are dry and hard and bitter and narrow, no church and no faith can save you from the judgment to come.

SP: So was religion rotten at the beginning; or has it become rotten?

ACD: Let us admit in the outset that every one of the fantastic beliefs which have been foisted upon mankind, has originally had some true and legitimate meaning, which has been exaggerated and deformed, until it has become a monstrosity.

SP: Perhaps an example would help.

ACD: Take the so-called sacrament of Confession.

SP: Ah yes – the practice of confessing your sins to a priest. 'Father, I have sinned.'

ACD: Indeed. And what could be more sensible or laudable than to take some elder of one's own sex into one's confidence and obtain his advice. The young man with an inclination to drink or debauchery is guided and gently reproved by his elder.

SP: Yes, I can see that.

ACD: But that out of this perfectly natural transaction, there should be so perverse and dangerous a practice that a young woman should tell her secret thoughts to a celibate of the opposite sex, is surely stark lunacy! It is difficult to say whether it is the man or the woman whose delicacy suffers most. If she must needs confess, then in the name of chastity and common sense, let it be to some discreet matron.

SP: They do say that tradition is truth pickled in history; and you're saying that everything is pickled; and nothing is fresh.

ACD: All vain forms must be discarded. But there is something to be added – something of infinite importance. We have to recognize that God, the Central source of all inspiration, has not ceased two thousand years ago to send his messages and his consolation to the world.

SP: You mean God is saying fresh things; but our love for tradition is making us deaf?

ACD: Through the movement which is called Spiritualism, we have learned that it is possible to get into touch with sources of knowledge which are far higher than ourselves, and thus to obtain a clear explanation of the reasons of our existence, and of the fate which awaits us after death. This is the most weighty message which has been sent out for two thousand years, and it has been received in the main with ignorant derision and contempt.

SP: So in your eyes, you didn't lose religion; religion lost itself.

ACD: Our religion has been like clay and gold; the clay of man-made dogma and observance; the gold of the inner spiritual meaning. The clay has long covered the gold, so that many of the most earnest of mankind have turned away heavy hearted, and never seen that the gold was there. Our task is to remove that clinging clay, and to expose and use the gold so that no man ever more can doubt its existence.

SP: Of course many in the church declare you to be a

destructive force.

ACD: I speak in a conservative and not in a destructive spirit. And anyway, I have my eyes fixed not upon the minority of this nation who belong to Christian churches, but to the majority who have been driven out of all communions by the fantastic out-of-date doctrines which are advanced, and who in their repulsion have now lost the essentials of religion.

SP: Those like yourself, in other words. And reading some of your comments, there's certainly little love lost between you and the *Old* Testament.

ACD: Witness a scheme depending upon a special tribal God, intensely anthropomorphic and filled with rage, jealousy and revenge. The conception pervades every book of the Old Testament. Even in the psalms, which are perhaps the most spiritual and beautiful section, the psalmist, amid much that is noble, sings of the fearsome things which his God will do to his enemies. 'Smite and spare not!' 'An eye for an eye!' How readily these texts spring to the grim lips of the murderous fanatic. Francis on St. Bartholomew's night, Alva in the Lowlands, Tilly at Magdeburg, Cromwell at Drogheda, the Covenanters at Philliphaugh, the Anabaptists of Munster and the early Mormons of Utah – they all found their murderous impulses fortified from this unholy source. Its red trail runs through history.

SP: So the Old Testament repels you; but Christ attracts you.

ACD: It is to be remembered that Christ's life in this world occupied, so far as we can estimate, 33 years; whilst from his arrest to his resurrection was less than a week. Yet the whole Christian system has come to revolve round his death, to the partial exclusion of the beautiful lesson of His life. Far too much weight has been placed upon the one, and far too little upon the other; for the death, beautiful and indeed perfect as it was, could be matched by that of many scores of thousands who have died for an idea; while the life, with its consistent record of charity, breadth of mind, unselfishness, courage, reason and progressiveness, is absolutely unique and superhuman. Even in these abbreviated, translated and second-hand records –

SP: You mean the Gospels?

ACD: Even in these we receive an impression such as no other life can give; an impression which fills us with utter reverence. Napoleon, no mean judge of human nature, said of it: 'It is different with Christ. Everything about him astonishes me. His spirit surprises me, and his will confounds me. Between him and anything of this world there is no possible comparison. He is really a being apart. The nearer I approach him and the closer I examine him, the more everything seems above me.'

SP: Powerful. That's not a testimony I'd heard before.

ACD: And it is this wonderful life – its example and inspiration – which was the real object of the descent of this high spirit on to our planet. If the human race had earnestly centred upon that, instead of losing itself in vain dreams of vicarious sacrifices and imaginary falls, with all the mystical and contentious philosophy which has centred round the subject – well, how very different the level of human culture and happiness would be to-day!

SP: And though you dismiss some of the church's claims about Jesus, you do make some claims of your own. For instance, I've never heard Jesus referred to as a medium before.

ACD: One cannot possibly understand many passages of

the New Testament unless he had a knowledge of psychical matters.

SP: How do you mean?

ACD: Take his words to the sick woman who touched him. 'Someone touched me,' he said, 'for I felt the strength go out of me.' This is exactly how a healing medium would feel.

SP: So we've just got Jesus wrong?

ACD: We were meant to use our reason and brains in adapting his teaching to the conditions of our altered lives and times.

SP: So these are different times to those of Christ and his words need translating?

ACD: Much that he said depended upon the society and mode of expression that belonged to his era.

SP: For instance?

ACD: Well, to suppose in these days that one has literally to give all to the poor; or that a starved English prisoner should literally love his enemy the Kaiser; or that because Christ protested against the lax marriages of his day, therefore two spouses who loathe each other should be for ever chained in a life servitude and martyrdom – all these assertions are to travesty his teaching and to take from it that robust quality of common sense which was its main characteristic. To ask what is impossible from human nature is to weaken your appeal when you ask for what is reasonable.

SP: But amidst your re-write of the gospel, you too can talk of something that surely underpins much religion – and that's God's loving kindness.

ACD: I see all around me things which show me the presence not merely of power, but of a very singular loving kindness, often in small matters.

SP: How do you mean?

ACD: There is the beauty of flowers and their scent. Every utilitarian object of life could be served without that. It fulfils no function. It seems an extra thrown in, out of kindness; a luxury among the necessities of life. So too the infinite variety of flavours.

SP: So there is some common ground between you and religion. And as I listen to you, my sense is that it isn't actually the old religions and philosophies that are most threatened by you. It's the new ones surely?

ACD: The answer is that to only one of these religions or philosophies is this new revelation absolutely fatal.

SP: And that one is?

ACD: Materialism. I do not say this in any spirit of hostility to materialists, who, so far as they are an organized body, are, I think, as earnest and moral as any other class. But the fact is manifest that if spirit can live without matter, then the foundation of materialism is gone; and the whole scheme of thought crashes to the ground.

FIVE

When the world went to war

*The Spiritualist movement – as it has come to be known –
emerged in America with the Fox sisters in the 1840's, but
travelled quickly to Great Britain, winning celebrity support
from writers like John Ruskin. By the 1880's, attempts at contact
with the dead was a common occurrence in Victorian parlours;
and it was during this decade that Doyle, while still a doctor in
Southsea, first attended séances. But just as the death toll of the
American Civil War intensified interest in the movement in The
States, so the death toll of the First World War heightened interest
in Great Britain.*

*Doyle had joined the Society for Psychical Research in 1882. But
it was only in 1919, a year after the death of his son Kingsley, that
he came out in public support for the spiritualist movement. The
horror and loss of war had changed the nature of the debate about
contact with the dead; it was suddenly more pressing and urgent.*

SP: You have never been one to minimize the significance
of the Great War, sir. You yourself witnessed the Battle of St
Quentin in 1916.

ACD: I will never forget the tangle of mutilated horses, their
necks arising and sinking, lying amidst the blood-soaked
remains of fallen soldiers.

SP: And in your opinion, has there ever been anything like it?

ACD: No. It has been our fate, among all the innumerable
generations of mankind, to face the most frightful calamity
that has ever befallen the world.

SP: And you don't want us to ignore this catastrophe; but

rather, to have our understanding enlarged by it?

ACD: There is a basic fact which cannot be denied, and should not be overlooked. For a most important deduction must immediately follow from it. That deduction is that we, who have borne the pains, shall also learn the lesson which they were intended to convey. If we do not learn it and proclaim it, then when can it ever be learned and proclaimed? Since there can never again be such a spiritual ploughing and harrowing and preparation for the seed.

SP: We must hope so.

ACD: And if our souls – wearied and tortured during those dreadful five years of self-sacrifice and suspense – can show no radical changes, then what souls will ever respond to a fresh influx of heavenly inspiration? In that case, the state of the human race would indeed be hopeless, and never in all the coming centuries would there be any prospect of improvement.

SP: So we must not avert our eyes, and make as if it never happened. Rather, the war is a moment to be seized.

ACD: The shock of the war was meant to rouse us to mental and moral earnestness; to give us the courage to tear away venerable shams, and to force the human race to realize and use the vast new revelation which has been so clearly stated and so abundantly proved, for all who will examine the statements and proofs with an open mind.

SP: Can I raise something here, Sir Arthur? For sometimes your implication appears to be that before your new message came along, everything was bad. But this simply isn't true.

ACD: We cannot deny that there has been much virtue, much gentleness and much spirituality in individuals. But the

39

churches were empty husks, which contained no spiritual food for the human race, and had in the main ceased to influence its actions, save in the direction of soulless forms. And this is not an over-coloured picture. Can we not see, then, what was the inner reason for the war?

SP: You believe there was a higher reason for the war; a reason above the normal reason which is the lunacy of humans when given power.

ACD: Can we not understand that it was needful to shake mankind loose from gossip and pink teas and sword-worship and Saturday night drunks and self-seeking politics and theological quibbles – to wake them up and make them realize that they stand upon a narrow knife-edge between two awful eternities, and that, here and now, they have to finish with make-beliefs; and instead, with real earnestness and courage, face those truths which have always been palpable where indolence or cowardice or vested interests have not obscured the vision.

SP: If it was a wake-up call, it was a savage one; and one which makes it hard to distinguish right from wrong. For you claim this evil was good?

ACD: Right and wrong are both tools which are being wielded by those great hands which are shaping the destinies of the universe; and both are making for improvements. The action of the one is immediate, and that of the other more slow; but none the less certain. Our own distinction of right and wrong is founded too much on the immediate convenience of the community, and does not enquire sufficiently deeply into the ultimate effect.

SP: I've heard you talking in similar ways about nature and evolution; that here too there is 'good savagery'.

ACD: It seems to me that Nature, still working on the lines of evolution, strengthens the race in two ways. The one is by improving those who are morally strong, which is done by increasing knowledge and broadening religious views.

SP: And the other?

ACD: The other, and hardly less important, is by the killing off and extinction of those who are morally weak. This is accomplished by drink and immorality.

SP: So The Four Horsemen of the Apocalypse are replaced by Two Horsemen – drink and immorality!

ACD: These are really two of the most important forces which work for the ultimate perfection of the human race. Looked at in one's own day, one can only see that they produce degradation and misery. But at the end of a third generation from then, what has happened? The line of the drunkard and the debauchee, physically as well as morally weakened, is either extinct or on the way towards it. A majority of drunkards never perpetuate their species at all.

SP: Strong words, Sir Arthur; you seem to speak with feeling on this matter.

He looks straight through me, which flusters me a little.

SP: But to return to the darkness with which we started, the War – whatever interest you had taken in the spiritualist movement before it, your attitude clearly changed as a result of it. The message found a home in you, and in 1919, you came out in public support of spiritualism for the first time. Was there a particular reason?

ACD: In the presence of an agonized world, hearing every day of the deaths of the flower of our race in the first promise of their unfulfilled youth; seeing around one the wives and the mothers who had no clear conception whither their loved ones had gone to – I seemed suddenly to see that this subject with which I had so long dallied was not merely a study of a force outside the rules of science, but that it was really something tremendous, a breaking down of the walls between two worlds; a direct undeniable call from beyond; a call of hope and guidance to the human race at the time of its deepest affliction.

SP: And of course your *own* deepest affliction, Sir Arthur. You lost nine family members in the war, and in particular, your dear brother Innes, and your dear son, Kingsley.

ACD: The objective side of spiritualism ceased to interest, for having made up one's mind that it was true, there was an end to the matter. The religious side of it was clearly of infinitely greater importance.

SP: And what religious answer did it give?

ACD: The answer is tidings of great joy. Of the new vital message to humanity nothing is more important than that – tidings of great joy.

SIX

The extraordinary case of the great Houdini

Doyle's friendship with Harry Houdini started as a transatlantic correspondence; with both keen to test the foundations of the spiritualist movement. They eventually met after Houdini performed in Brighton on his tour of Great Britain. Doyle was impressed and baffled by the skill of his performance. He invited Houdini to his home, and also arranged for him to experience over a hundred séances in Britain. In return, Houdini claimed he had seen trickery at each and every one.

It was a friendship that was to become increasingly tested. Here were two men pulling in very different directions.

SP: Sir Arthur, you believe Harry Houdini was the greatest physical medium of modern times.

ACD: I do not see how it can ever now be finally and definitely proved, but circumstantial evidence may be very strong, as Thoreau said when he found a trout in the milk jug. I foresee that the subject will be debated for many years to come, so perhaps my opinion, since I knew him well, and always entertained this possibility in my mind, may be of interest.

SP: Indeed.

ACD: Let me say, in the first instance, that in a long life which has touched every side of humanity, Houdini is far and away the most curious and intriguing character whom I have ever encountered.

SP: Why so?

ACD: I have met better men, and I have certainly met very

many worse ones; but I have never met a man who had such strange contrasts in his nature, and whose actions and motives it was more difficult to foresee or to reconcile.

SP: Good and bad?

ACD: Yes, and I will first, as is only proper, dwell upon the great good that lay in his nature. He had the essential masculine quality of courage to a supreme degree. Nobody has ever done, and nobody in all human probability will ever do, such reckless feats of daring. His whole life was one long succession of them, and when I say that amongst them was the leaping from one aeroplane to another, with handcuffed hands at the height of three thousand feet, one can form an idea of the extraordinary lengths that he would go.

SP: Almost superhuman.

ACD: In this, however, as in much more that concerned him, there was a certain psychic element that he was ready to admit freely.

SP: How do you mean?

ACD: He told me that a voice, which was independent of his own reason or judgment, told him what to do and how to do it. So long as he obeyed the voice he was assured of safety. 'It all comes as easy as stepping off a log,' he said to me, 'but I have to wait for the voice. You stand there before a jump, swallowing the yellow stuff that everyman has in him. Then at last you hear the voice and you jump. Once I jumped on my own and I nearly broke my neck.' This was the nearest admission that I ever had from him that I was right in thinking that there was a psychic element which was essential to every one of his feats.

SP: So a man of great courage and psychic awareness. What else?

ACD: Apart from his amazing courage, he was remarkable for his cheery urbanity in everyday life. One could not wish for a better companion so long as one was with him – though he might do and say the most unexpected things when one was absent. He was, like most Jews, estimable in his family relationships. His love for his dead mother seemed to be the ruling passion of his life, which he expressed on all sorts of public occasions in a way which was, I am sure, sincere, but is strange to our colder Western blood.

SP: People rarely express their honest feelings about their parents.

ACD: And there were many things in Houdini which were as Oriental as there were in our own Disraeli. He was devoted also to his wife, and with good reason, for she was as devoted to him; but again, his intimacy showed itself in unconventional ways. When in his examination before the Senatorial Committee he was hard-pressed by some defender of Spiritualism who impugned his motives in his violent and vindictive campaign against mediums, his answer was to turn to his wife and to say, 'I have always been a good boy, have I not?'

SP: Sounds to me like he was a little boy looking for a mother's approval.

ACD: Another favourable side of his character was his charity. I have heard, and am quite prepared to believe, that he was the last refuge of the down-and-out, especially if he belonged to his own profession of showman. This charity extended even beyond the grave, and if he heard of any old magician whose tombstone needed repair he took it upon himself at once to set the matter right. One man embraced him in the street, and upon Houdini angrily demanding who the devil he was, he answered, "Why, I am the man whose rent you have paid for the last ten years."

sp: That's a nice story.

acd: And he was devoted to children, though he had none of his own. He was never too busy to give a special free performance for the youngsters. At Edinburgh he was so shocked at the bare feet of the kiddies that he had them all into the theatre, and fitted them then and there with five hundred pairs of boots. He was the greatest publicity agent that ever lived, however, so that it is not ill-natured to surmise that the local papers had been advised beforehand, and that the advertisement was well worth it.

sp: So a fine list of virtues. But what of his other side? Every scale has two bowls.

acd: A prevailing feature of his character was a vanity which was so obvious and childish that it became more amusing than offensive. I can remember, for example, that when he introduced his brother to me, he did it by saying, 'This is the brother of the great Houdini.' This without any twinkle of humour and in a perfectly natural manner! And this enormous vanity was combined with a passion for publicity which knew no bounds, and which must at all costs be gratified. There was no consideration of any sort that would restrain him if he saw his way to an advertisement.

sp: So he needed to be out there; he needed to be in front of people. He dreaded the silence.

acd: Even when he laid flowers upon the graves of the dead it was in the prearranged presence of the local photographers.

And it was this desire to play a constant public part that had a great deal to do with his furious campaign against spiritualism. He knew that the public took a keen interest in the matter, and that there was unlimited publicity to be had from it.

SP: So what form did this campaign take?

ACD: His favourite argument, and that of many of his fellow-conjurers, was this flourishing of dollar-wads. It is obviously absurd, since the money will only be paid if you satisfy the challenger; and since the challenger has to pay the money, he naturally never will be satisfied!

SP: So spiritualists are asked for 'proof' – but it's the challenger who decides what constitutes proof. And nothing ever quite does, so the money is safe.

ACD: The classical instance is that of the *Scientific American* magazine, which offered a large sum for any well-attested psychic phenomenon, but on being confronted with the Crandon phenomena – which are perhaps the best attested in the whole annals of psychical research – found reasons for withholding the money.

SP: Crafty.

ACD: And I remember that when I arrived in New York, Houdini offered some huge sum that he could do anything which I had ever seen a medium do. I at once accepted his challenge, and proposed as a test that he should materialize the face of my mother in such a way that others besides myself, who had known her in life, could recognize it. I heard no more of the matter after that – and yet in England a medium had actually done this! I would have brought my witnesses across the Atlantic had the test been accepted.

SP: Yet you can see why he was suspicious. In the States, even more than in England, there were a lot of frauds.

ACD: I admit that I underrated the corruption in the States. What first brought it home to me was that my friend Mrs. Crandon told me that she had received price lists from some firm which manufactures fraudulent instruments for performing tricks. If such a firm can make a living, there must be some villainy about, and a more judicious Houdini might well find a useful field of activity. It is these hyenas who retard our progress. I have myself had a hand in exposing more than one of them.

SP: You have exposed a good number in your time, I know. But Houdini wanted to declare everyone a fake.

ACD: I did advise Houdini.

SP: What did you say?

ACD: I said, 'I see that you know a great deal about the negative side of spiritualism – I hope more on the positive side will come your way!' But it wants to be approached not in the spirit of a detective approaching a suspect, but in that of a humble religious soul, yearning for help and comfort.

SP: I suspect that was never going to be Houdini's way.

ACD: No.

SP: Though judging from an entry in his diary, he was impressed by your commitment to the cause. If I may read the entry: 'Visited Sir Arthur Conan Doyle at Crowborough. Met Lady Doyle and the three children. Had lunch with them. They believe implicitly in spiritualism. Sir Arthur told me he had spoken six times to his son. No possible chance for trickery. Lady Doyle also believes and has had tests that are beyond belief. Told them all to me.' He may be keeping his own opinions to himself, but he clearly feels the force of yours.

ACD: I think he did.

SP: And then, of course, that important incident in your relationship: when you believed that you actually made contact with his dead mother in a séance, through your wife's gift of automatic writing. He records the words his mother spoke:

ACD: Yes. 'Oh my darling, thank God, thank God, at last I'm through – I've tried, oh so often – now I am happy. Why of course I want to talk to my boy – my own beloved boy – Friends, thank you with all my heart for this!'

SP: But Houdini wasn't impressed for then he adds: 'Message written by Lady Doyle claiming the spirit of my dear mother had control of her hand – my sainted mother could not write English and spoke broken English.' He then rubbished you in the New York papers. How did you feel about that?

ACD: I had no fancy for sparring with a friend in public, so I took no notice. But nonetheless, I felt rather sore about it.

SP: And then there was the Crandon case, which you believe not only exposed him; but had darker consequences still.

ACD: He had become familiar in advance with the procedure of the Crandon circle, and with the types of phenomena. It was easy for him to lay his plans.

SP: He wished to make the medium, Mrs Crandon, look stupid.

ACD: Indeed. But what he failed to take into account was the presiding spirit, Walter.

SP: Walter was the dead brother of Mrs Crandon.

ACD: He was the dead brother of Mrs. Crandon, a very real and live entity, who was by no means inclined to allow his innocent sister to be made the laughing stock of the continent. And it was the unseen Walter who checkmated the carefully laid plans of the magician.

SP: Sounds intriguing. So what happened?

ACD: The account of what occurred I take from the notes which were taken by the circle at the time. The first phenomenon to be tested was the ringing of an electric bell which could only be done by pressing down a flap of wood, well out of the reach of the medium. The room was darkened, but the bell did not ring. Suddenly the angry voice of Walter was heard.

'You have put something to stop the bell ringing, Houdini, you blackguard!' he cried.

Walter has a wealth of strong language and makes no pretence at all to be a very elevated being. They all have their use over there. On this occasion, at least, the use was evident, for when the light was turned up, there was the rubber from the end of a pencil stuck into the angle of the flap in such a way as to make it impossible that it could descend and press the bell.

SP: And Walter believed Houdini had put it there?

ACD: Houdini professed complete ignorance as to how it got there, but who else had the deft touch to do such a thing in the dark; and why was it only in his presence that such a thing occurred? It is clear that if he could say afterwards, when he had quietly removed the rubber, that his arrival had made all further trickery impossible, he would have scored the first trick in the game.

SP: Yes, I can see that.

ACD: He should have taken warning and realized that he was up against powers which were too strong for him, and which might prove dangerous if provoked too far. However, much worse was to come.

SP: Houdini had further plans?

ACD: The lady was put into a reconstituted box, her arms protruding through holes on each side. Houdini was then observed without any apparent reason, to pass his hand along the lady's arm and so into the box. Presently, the lady's arms were placed inside and the attempt was to be made to ring the bell-box while only her head projected. Suddenly the terrible Walter intervened.

'Houdini, you blackguard!' he thundered. 'You have put a rule into the cabinet. You blackguard! Remember, Houdini, you won't live forever. Someday you've got to die.'

Well, the lights were turned on, of course, and, shocking to relate, a two-foot folding rule was found lying in the box. It was a most deadly trick, for, of course, if the bell had rung, Houdini would have demanded a search of the cabinet, and the rule would have been found. It would, if held between the teeth, have enabled the medium to have reached and pressed down the flap of the bell-box, and all America would have resounded next day with the astuteness of Houdini and the proven villainy of the Crandons!

SP: So what happened after Walter shouted out?

ACD: For the moment Houdini was completely overcome, and cowered, as well he might before the wrath of the unseen. But one of Houdini's characteristics was that nothing in this world or the next could permanently abash him.

SP: He had no shame?

ACD: Incredible as it may seem, he had his advertisement after all, for he flooded America with a pamphlet to say that he had shown that the Crandons were frauds, and that he had in some unspecified way exposed them. Speaking with a full knowledge, I say that this incident was never an exposure of anyone but Houdini, and is a most serious blot upon his career.

SP: You have suggested this incident had dark consequences?

ACD: The Crandons are themselves the most patient and forgiving people in the world, treating the most irritating opposition with a good-humoured and amused tolerance. But there are other forces which are beyond human control, and from that day the shadow lay heavy upon Houdini.

SP: How do you mean?

ACD: His anti-spiritualist agitation became more and more unreasoning until it bordered upon a mania, which could only be explained in some quarters by supposing that he was in the pay of certain clerical fanatics – an accusation which I do not believe. It is true that in order to preserve some show of reason, he proclaimed that he wished only to attack dishonest mediums, but as in the same breath he would assert that there were no honest ones, his moderation was more apparent than real! If he had consulted the reports of the National Association of American Spiritualists, he would have found that this representative body was far more efficient in exposing those swindlers than he had ever been, for they had the necessary experience by which the true can be separated from the false.

SP: And you say that his death was foreseen by various people; a judgement even?

ACD: There were some remarkable points about his death. It seems that upon Friday, October 22nd, he was lying in his dressing room, reading his letters. It was about five in the afternoon. He had lectured at McGill University a few days before, and with his usual affability, he allowed some of the students to come in and see him. What followed may be taken verbatim from the report of one of these young men.

'Houdini,' he says, 'was facing us and lying down on a couch at the time reading some mail, his right side nearest us. This first-year student engaged Houdini more or less continually in a conversation, whilst my friend Mr. Smilovitch continued to sketch Houdini. This student was the first to raise the question of Houdini's strength. My friend and I were not so much interested in his strength as we were in his mental acuteness, his skill, his beliefs and his personal experiences. Houdini stated that he had extraordinary muscles in his forearms, in his shoulders and in his back; and he asked all of us present to feel them, which we did.

The first-year McGill student then asked Houdini whether it was true that punches in the stomach did not hurt him. Houdini remarked rather unenthusiastically that his stomach could resist much; although he did not speak of it in superlative terms.

SP: I think I know what happened next.

ACD: 'Thereupon he gave Houdini some very hammer-like

blows below the belt, first securing Houdini's permission to strike him. Houdini was reclining at the time with his right side nearest Whitehead; and the said student was more or less bending over him. These blows fell on that part of the stomach to the right of the navel, and were struck on the side nearest us, which was in fact Houdini's right side; I do not remember exactly how many blows were struck. I am certain, however, of at least four very hard and severe body blows, because at the end of the second or third blow, I verbally protested against this sudden onslaught on the part of this first-year student, using the words, 'Hey there. You must be crazy, what are you doing?' or words to that effect. But Whitehead continued striking Houdini with all his strength.

Houdini stopped him suddenly in the midst of a punch, with a gesture that he had had enough. At the time Whitehead was striking Houdini, the latter looked as though he was in extreme pain and winced as each blow was struck.

Houdini immediately after stated that he had had no opportunity to prepare himself against the blows, as he did not think that Whitehead would strike him as suddenly as he did and with such force; and that he would have been in a better position to prepare for the blows if he had arisen from his couch for this purpose. But the injury to his foot prevented him from getting about rapidly.'

SP: So that's what killed Houdini?

ACD: There is no doubt that the immediate cause of the death was a ruptured appendix, and it was certified as traumatic appendicitis by all three doctors who attended him. It is, however, a very rare complaint, one of the doctors asserting that he had never seen a case before. When one considers how often boxers are struck violent blows in this region, one can understand that it is not usually so vulnerable. From the time that he reached hospital, he seems to have known that he was doomed.

SP: Now Sir Arthur, you believe that Houdini had super-human powers, through secret knowledge from inner voices. Most will disagree with you; most will say he was just a very great magician.

ACD: I am aware that Houdini really was a very skilful conjurer. All that could be known in that direction he knew. Thus he confused the public mind by mixing up things which were dimly within their comprehension with things which were beyond anyone's comprehension.

SP: Many did similar tricks to him.

ACD: I am aware that there is a box trick, and that there is a normal handcuff and bag trick. But these are not in the same class with Houdini's work. I will believe they are when I see one of these other gentlemen thrown in a box off London Bridge. One poor man in America actually believed these explanations, and on the strength of them, jumped in a weighted packing case into a river in the Middle West; and one did so in Germany. They are there yet!

SP: Are you sure that this is not you wishing to believe it were so?

ACD: I will take a single case of Houdini's powers, and of the sort of thing that he would say, in order to show you what he is up against if he means to maintain that these tricks had no abnormal element.

SP: Fair enough.

ACD: The description is by my friend, Captain Bartlett,

himself a man of many accomplishments, psychic and otherwise. In the course of their conversation he said to his guest:

'How about your box trick?'

Instantly Houdini's expression changed. The sparkle left his eyes and his face looked drawn and haggard. 'I cannot tell you,' he said, in a low, tense voice. 'I don't know myself, and, what is more, I have always a dread lest I should fail, and then I would not live. I have promised Mrs. Houdini to give up the box trick at the end of the season, for she makes herself ill with anxiety, and for myself I shall be relieved too.'

He stooped to stroke our cats, and to our amazement, they fled from the room with their tails in the air – and for some minutes they dashed wildly up and down stairs, scattering the mats in all directions.

SP: So the cats were spooked! But other conjurers do not bestow special powers on him.

ACD: The attempts upon the part of his brother-magicians to give some sort of explanation of Houdini's feats only serve to deepen the mystery. Mr. Howard Thurston, for whose opinion I have respect, for he seemed to me to be the only American conjurer who had some real accurate knowledge of psychic matters, says that his feats all come within the power of advanced conjuring.

SP: And that's my point.

ACD: I know that feats with the same name do so, but I venture to express the opinion that such feats as Houdini did, have never been explained and are in an altogether different class. Houdini was one of the most remarkable men of whom we have any record, and he will live in history with such personalities as Cagliostro, the Chevalier D' Eon and other strange characters. He had many outstanding qualities, and the world is the poorer for his loss. As matters stand, no one can say positively and finally that his powers were abnormal –

SP: No

ACD: But you will, I hope, agree with me that there is a case to be answered.

SEVEN

Ghost writing for Oscar Wilde

Sir Arthur had met Oscar Wilde in the summer of 1889 when both were invited to dinner by the American publisher J. M. Stoddart – the one who thought Doyle looked like 'a walrus in Sunday clothes'. They met together at the Langham Hotel in Portland Place, London. Apparently Oscar, then aged 35, and Doyle, aged 30, got on very well, discussing Doyle's recent historical novel, 'Micah Clarke'. Oscar was in fine conversational form and Doyle was impressed and charmed: 'It was indeed a golden evening for me,' he recalled.

*It was a dinner which ended with Doyle being commissioned to write another Sherlock Holmes adventure (*The Sign of Four*) and Wilde commissioned to write* The Picture of Dorian Gray. *If only all publishers lunches were so productive!*

Wilde famously said that he put his talent into his work and his genius into his life. He died in 1900, which strangely, is where this story about him begins...

ACD: From time to time communications have come through mediums which are alleged to emanate from men who have been famous in literature.

SP: So a literary giant continues their output from beyond the grave? Publishers should be delighted.

ACD: These writings have been set aside by the ordinary critic, who starts with the assumption that the thing is in a general sense absurd, and therefore applies the same judgment with little or no examination to the particular case. Those of us, however, who have found that many psychic claims have actually been made good, may be inclined to look a little more closely into these compositions, and judge how far, from internal evidence, the alleged authorship is possible or absurd.

SP: If what you say is true, Sir Arthur, are we to expect a sequel to Macbeth any day now? I mean, I wish to remain open, but I can see why critics are suspicious.

ACD: I venture to say that an impartial critic who approached the subject from this angle will be rather surprised at the result.

SP: So how are these messages received?

ACD: The messages, it should be explained, come partly by automatic writing, while in a normal state; and partly by the ouija board. Mrs. Dowden was associated with Mr. Soal in the experiments. She sometimes worked alone, and sometimes with his hands upon the ouija board.

SP: And they claim to have heard from your friend Oscar Wilde. Do you have any examples of Wildean writing from the other side?

ACD: Here are some of the messages which seem to me to be most characteristic of Wilde's personality and literary style.

SP: Should be interesting.

ACD: 'In eternal twilight I move, but I know that in the world there is day and night, seedtime and harvest, and red sunset must follow apple-green dawn. Every year, spring throws her green veil over the world and the red autumn glory comes to mock the yellow moon. Already the may is creeping like a white mist over land and hedgerow, and year after year the hawthorn bears blood-red fruit after the death of its may.'

SP: It's good writing.

ACD: This is not merely adequate Wilde. It is exquisite Wilde. It is so beautiful that it might be chosen for special inclusion in any anthology of his writings. The adjective 'apple-green' for dawn; and the picture of the may 'creeping like a white mist' are two highlights in a brilliant passage, with such a quick response to colour. It is not too much to say that the posthumous Wilde in such passages as this, is Wilde with an added sparkle.

SP: You mean Wilde has improved with death? So what came next from the great man?

ACD: Wilde was then subjected to a long questionnaire, which he answered with great precision. When asked why he came, he answered:

'To let the world know that Oscar Wilde is not dead. His thoughts live on in the hearts of all those who in a gross age can hear the flute voice of beauty calling on the hills; or mark where her white feet brush the dew from the cowslips in the morning. Now the mere memory of the beauty of the world is an exquisite pain. I was always one of those for whom the visible world existed. I worshipped at the shrine of things seen. There was not a blood stripe on a tulip or a curve on a shell, or a tone on the sea, but had for me its meaning and its mystery, and its appeal to the imagination. Others might sip the pale lees of the cup of thought, but for me the red wine of life.'

This also is beautiful and rare literary work.

SP: I agree.

ACD: If an artist can tell a Rubens by its colouring or a sculptor can assign an ancient statue to Phidias, then I claim that a man with an adequate sense of the rhythm of good prose can ascribe these fine extracts to Wilde and to no one else. His hallmark is stamped upon them for all the world to see, and when it ceases to turn away its head, it will see it clearly enough. Immersed in trivialities, it seems to have no leisure at present for the great questions of life and of death.

SP: And how exactly did these pieces of writing appear?

ACD: These two beautiful passages and several others almost as fine, came in a single sitting on June 8th, 1923, and were produced by Mr Soal writing, while Mrs Dowden laid her hand upon his. In many forms of mediumship, it is to be observed that the blending of two human atmospheres produces finer results than either alone can get.

SP: And what about Wilde's humour? Do we get a taste of that from beyond the grave? There's always been some debate about whether humour survives.

ACD: The cynical humour of Wilde, and a certain mental arrogance which was characteristic, does break out in these passages.

SP: An example?

ACD: 'Being dead is the most boring experience in life. That is if one excepts being married, or dining with a schoolmaster.'

SP: Boom, boom!

ACD: Again, being dissatisfied with one of his own images, he writes, 'Stop! Stop! This image is insufferable. You write like a successful grocer who, from selling pork, has taken to writing poetry.' And when someone alluded to an occasion when Whistler had scored off him, he wrote, 'With James vulgarity always begins at home.'

SP: It's certainly hard to see Mr Soal and Mrs Dowden coming up with these lines; unless they had a script writer under the table.

ACD: And again, 'I do not wish to burden you with details of my life, which was like a candle that had guttered at the end. I rather wish to make you believe that I was the medium through which beauty filtered, and was distilled like the essence of a rose.'

SP: Well, it's all good stuff. And doesn't he comment on Yeats?

ACD: Yes. His literary criticism was acid and unjust, but witty.

'I knew Yeats well,' he says, 'a fantastical mind, but so full of inflated joy in himself that his little cruse of poetry was erupted early in his career; a little drop of beauty which was spread only with infinite pains over the span of many years.'

SP: Pretty damning, yes.

ACD: Can anyone contend that both Mr Soal and Mrs Dowden have a hidden strand in their own personality which enables them on occasion to write like a great deceased writer; and at the same time a want of conscience which permits that subconscious strand to actually claim that it 'is' the deceased author? Such an explanation would seem infinitely more unlikely than any transcendental one can do.

SP: I'm reminded of Sherlock Holmes' advice to Watson in '*The Sign of Four*. 'How often have I said to you, Watson, that when you have eliminated the impossible, whatever remains, however improbable, must be the truth.'

ACD: The case might be made fairly convincing on the question of style alone. But there is much more in it than that. The actual writing – which was done at a speed which forbids conscious imitation – is often the handwriting of Wilde, and reproduces certain curious little tricks of spacing which were usual with him in life. He alludes freely to all sorts of episodes, many of them little known, which have been shown to be actual facts. He gives criticisms of authors with a sure, but rather unkind touch, where the medium has little or no acquaintance with the writings criticized. He alludes to people whom he has known in life with the utmost facility. In the case of one, Mrs. Chan Toon, the name was so unlikely that it seemed to me that there must be some mistake. As if to resolve my doubts, a letter reached me presently from the very lady herself!

SP: So you genuinely believe that it is Wilde speaking from the grave?

ACD: I do not think that any person who approached this problem with an open mind can doubt that the case for Wilde's survival and communication is an overpoweringly strong one. The Oscar Wilde transcripts are the best evidence for the survival of personality that I know of.

EIGHT

The case book of the psychic detective

Sir Arthur Conan Doyle became a national treasure by creating the brilliant character of Sherlock Holmes. Here was a figure at once light and dark. One who dabbled in cocaine; excelled in deduction and played the violin. He was called in by governments when the matter was too sensitive or too tricky for the police force; had a passion for disguise, a genius for logic and wrote a monograph on the different types of cigar ash. Women begged for his help; but there was never romance; always the gentleman, yet always unknown.

When Sir Arthur finally laid Sherlock to rest, one might have thought the detective stories were over. But this was not the case; for after Sherlock came the psychic detectives, who found their answers from beyond the grave. Those of a nervous disposition might wish to leave this chapter well alone.

SP: Your interest in detection didn't stop with Holmes, Sir Arthur. You know of a story in which it is the ghosts who lead the living to the awful truth.

ACD: In this very dramatic case a lady with her children occupied a lonely house upon the Cornish coast.

SP: A good setting for a murder mystery.

ACD: She was much disturbed by a ghostly visitor who passed with a heavy tread up the stairs at a certain hour of the night, disappearing into a panel in the landing.

SP: Are you sure this isn't a Sherlock Holmes?

ACD: The lady had the courage to lie in wait for him, and

perceived him to be a small, aged man in a shabby tweed suit, carrying his boots in his hand. He emitted 'a sort of yellow luminous light.' This creature ascended at 1 a.m., and emerged again at 4.30, descending the stair with the same audible tread. The lady kept the matter to herself, but a nurse who was brought to tend one of the children came screaming in the middle of the night, to say that there was 'a dreadful old man' in the house.

SP: So she'd seen the same man?

ACD: That's right. She had descended to the dining room to get some water for her patient, and had seen the old man seated in a chair and taking off his boots. He was seen by his own light, for she had not had time to strike a match. The lady's brother and her husband both corroborated the phenomena, and the latter went very thoroughly into the matter.

SP: And what did he find?

ACD: He found that under the house was a cellar which opened into a cave, up which the water came at full tide. It was an ideal situation for a smuggler. That night the husband and wife kept watch in the cellar, where they saw a very terrible spectacle. In a light resembling that of the moon, they were aware of two elderly men engaged in a terrific struggle. One got the other down and killed him, bundling the body through the door into the cave beyond. He then buried the knife with which the deed was done, though curiously enough this detail was only observed by the husband, who actually unearthed a knife afterwards at the spot.

SP: Go on.

ACD: Both witnesses then saw the murderer pass them, and

they followed him into the dining room, where he drank some brandy, though this action was seen by the wife and not the husband. He then took off his boots, exactly as the nurse had already described. With his boots in his hand he ascended the stairs and passed through the panel as he had done so often before – the inference being that on each previous occasion, the scene in the cellar had preceded his advent.

SP: Intriguing.

ACD: Inquiry now showed that many years ago the house had been inhabited by two brothers who amassed considerable wealth by smuggling. They had hoarded their money in partnership, but one of them finally announced his intention of getting married, which involved his drawing his share of the treasure. Soon afterwards, this brother disappeared, and it was rumoured that he had gone to sea upon a long voyage. So far as I remember – for I speak with only notes of the episode before me – the other brother went mad, and the affair was never cleared up in his lifetime.

SP: But the old man's ghost lived on; and nailed him as the murderer!

ACD: It should be added that the panel into which the vision disappeared concealed a large cupboard, which might well have been the treasure house of the establishment. The graphic touch of the boots carried in the hand suggests that there was some housekeeper or other resident who might be disturbed by the sound of the murderer's footsteps.

SP: And you say the ghost is visible to everyone.

ACD: In this case, one can certainly imagine that in so fratricidal a strife, there would be a peculiar intensity of emotion on the part of both the actors, which would leave a marked record if anything could do so.

SP: You mean the visibility of the ghost might be determined by the degree of emotion in the scene?

ACD: That the record was indeed very marked is shown by the fact that the sight was not reserved for people with psychic qualities, as is often the case; but that everyone, the husband, the wife and the nurse all saw the apparition, which must therefore have been particularly solid, even after the lapse of so many years. It might, I think, be put forward as a hypothesis that the permanency and solidity of the form depend upon the extremity of the emotion.

SP: Well, it's a remarkable case. And the natural question now arises: If you have spirit communications, why are you sometimes unable to get an explanation?

ACD: The answer is that spirit communication is also governed by inexorable laws; and that you might as well expect an electric current along a broken wire as to get a communication when the conditions have become impossible.

SP: This is interesting territory.

ACD: Well, passing on to a more definite example, let us take the case of the murder of Maria Marten, which was for a long time a favourite subject when treated at village fairs under the name of *The Mystery of the Red Barn*.

SP: Ah, well here you have my particular attention, because I myself, in my amateur dramatics days, once appeared in this melodrama. As I remember, for it was a while back, Maria Marten was murdered by a young farmer named Corder, who should have married her but failed to do so He killed her to conceal the result of their illicit union.

ACD: His ingenious method was to announce that he was about to marry the girl, and then at the last hour, he shot her dead and buried her body. He then disappeared from the neighbourhood, and gave out that he and she were secretly wedded and living together at some unknown address.

SP: The murder was on May 18, 1827, and for some time, Corder's plan was successful – the crime being effectively concealed because he'd left instructions that the barn should be filled up with stock.

ACD: The rascal sent home a few letters purporting to be from the Isle of Wight, explaining that Maria and he were living together in great contentment. Some suspicion was aroused by the fact that the postmarks of these letters were all from London –

SP: – a small oversight -

ACD: – but none the less the matter might have been overlooked had it not been for the unusual action of an obscure natural law which had certainly never been allowed for in Mr. Corder's calculations.

SP: What law was that?

ACD: Mrs. Marten, the girl's mother, dreamed upon three nights running that her daughter had been murdered.

SP: Now that I *didn't* know; though I suppose we all have odd dreams from time to time.

ACD: Yes, and this in itself might count for little, since as you say, it may have only reflected her vague fears and distrust. The dreams, however, were absolutely definite. She saw in them the red barn, and even the very spot in which the remains had been deposited. The latter detail is of great importance, since it disposes of the idea that the incident could have arisen from the girl having told her mother that she had an assignation there. The dreams occurred in March 1828, ten months after the crime, but it was the middle of April before the wife was able to persuade her husband to act upon such evidence.

s p: I can understand his reluctance.

a c d: At last she broke down his very natural scruples, however, and permission was given to examine the barn, now cleared of its contents. The woman pointed to the spot and the man dug. A piece of shawl was immediately exposed, and eighteen inches below it, the body itself was discovered – the horrified searcher staggering in frenzy out of the ill-omened barn. The dress, the teeth and some small details were enough to establish the identification.

s p: Amazing.

a c d: The villain was arrested in London, where he had become, by marriage, the proprietor of a girls' school, and was engaged, at the moment of capture, in ticking off the minutes for the correct boiling of the breakfast eggs.

s p: What happened to him?

a c d: He was duly hanged, confessing his guilt in a half-hearted way before his execution.

s p: So that was a case solved by a dream being given to a woman.

a c d: Yes, and take another case, involving a dream, which is perfectly authentic. Upon February 8th, 1840, Edmund Norway, the chief officer of the ship 'Orient,' at that time near

St. Helena, dreamed a dream between the hours of 10 p.m. and 4 a.m. in which he saw his brother Nevell, a Cornish gentleman, murdered by two men.

SP: Not a pleasant dream – to see your brother murdered. How did it happen?

ACD: His brother was seen to be mounted. One of the assailants caught the horse's bridle and snapped a pistol twice, but no report was heard. He and his comrade then struck him several blows, and dragged him to the side of the road, where they left him. The road appeared to be a familiar one in Cornwall, but the house, which should have been on the right, came out upon the left in the visual picture. The dream was recorded in writing at the time, and was told to the other officers of the ship.

SP: And I think I can guess what then happened.

ACD: Yes, the murder had actually occurred, and the assassins, two brothers named Lightfoot, were executed on April 13th of that year, at Bodmin. In his confession the elder brother said: 'I went to Bodmin on February 8th and met my brother. My brother knocked Mr. Norway down. He snapped a pistol at him twice, but it did not go off. He then knocked him down with the pistol. It was on the road to Wade-bridge' (the road which had been seen in the dream). 'We left the body in the water on the left side of the road coming to Wadebridge. My brother drew the body across the road to the watering.' The evidence made it clear that the murder was committed between the hours of ten and eleven at night, and as St. Helena is, roughly, in the same longitude as England, the time of the dream might exactly correspond with that of the crime.

SP: So he dreamed the event as it was happening?

ACD: It can easily be conceived that the consciousness of the sailor, drawn to his brother by recent loving thoughts, went swiftly to him in his sleep, and was so shocked to witness his murder, that it was able to carry the record through into his normal memory. The case would resolve itself, then, into one which depended upon the normal but unexplored powers of the human organism, and not upon any interposition from the spirit of the murdered man. Had the vision of the latter appeared alone, without the accompanying scene, it would have seemed more probable that it was indeed a post-mortem apparition.

SP: So can these paranormal forces be turned to good use? I mean should every police station have a resident psychic?

ACD: It would be a degradation to use these forces for purely material ends, and it would, in my opinion, bring some retribution with it; but, where the interests of justice are concerned, I am convinced that they could indeed be used to good effect. Here is a case in point. Two brothers, Eugene and Paul Dupont, lived some fifty years ago in the Rue St. Honoré of Paris.

SP: The City of love! Though not, I suspect, in this story.

ACD: Eugene was a banker, Paul a man of letters. Eugene disappeared. Every conceivable effort was made to trace him, but the police finally gave it up as hopeless.

SP: They'd reached a dead end.

ACD: Paul was persevering, however, and in company with a friend, Laporte, he visited Mme. Huerta, a well-known clairvoyant, and asked for her assistance.

SP: Any port in a storm, I suppose.

ACD: Mme. Huerta, in the mesmerized state, very quickly got in touch with the past of the two brothers, from the dinner where they had last met. She described Eugene, and followed his movements from the hour that he left the restaurant until he vanished into a house which was identified without difficulty by her audience. She then described how inside the house Eugene Dupont had held a conference with two men whom she described; how he had signed some paper and had received a bundle of bank notes. She then saw him leave the house, she saw the two men follow him, she saw two other men join in the pursuit, and finally she saw the four assault the banker, murder him and throw the body into the Seine.

SP: Remarkable, if it was true. But did anyone believe her?

ACD: Paul was convinced by the narrative, but his comrade, Laporte, regarded it as a fabrication. They had no sooner reached home, however, than they learned that the missing man had been picked out of the river and was exposed at the Morgue.

SP: So now the police were interested again.

ACD: The police were inclined to take the view of suicide, as a good deal of money was in the pockets. Paul Dupont knew better, however. He hunted out the house; he discovered that the occupants did business with his brother's firm; he found that they held a receipt for two thousand pounds in exchange for notes paid to his brother on the night of the crime; and yet those notes were missing. A letter making an appointment was also discovered.

SP: The net was closing.

ACD: The two men, a father and son, named Dubuchet, were then arrested, and the missing links were at once discovered.

The pocket book which Eugene Dupont had in his possession on the night of the murder was found in Dubuchet's bureau. Other evidence was forthcoming, and finally the two villains were found guilty and were condemned to penal servitude for life.

SP: And what of the medium, Mme. Huerta?

ACD: The medium was not summoned as a witness, on the grounds that she was not conscious at the time of her vision; but her revelations undoubtedly brought about the discovery of the crime.

SP: That is plain enough.

ACD: And it is clear in this authentic case that the police would have saved themselves much trouble, and come to a swifter conclusion, had they themselves consulted Mme. Huerta in the first instance.

SP: True.

ACD: And if it is obviously true in this case, why might it not be so in many other cases? It should be possible at every great police-centre to have the call upon the best clairvoyant or other medium that can be got, and to use them freely, for what they are worth. None are infallible. They have their off-days and their failures. No man should ever be convicted upon their evidence. But when it comes to suggesting clues and links, then it might be invaluable.

SP: These are remarkable cases you have described, Sir Arthur. But like any apparent miracle, they raise more questions than they answer. For if these innocent victims have been helped by powers beyond our comprehension, why haven't these powers saved other innocents? Any criminologist knows dozens of cases where innocent men and women have gone to the scaffold.

ACD: Why were they not saved? I have spoken and written in vain if I have not by now enabled you to answer the question yourself. If the physical means are not there, then it is impossible. It may seem unjust, but not more so than the fact that a ship provided with wireless may save its passengers, while another is heard of no more.

NINE

The author away with the fairies

At the end of the 19ᵗʰ century, Arthur Conan Doyle was a figure most men would have liked to emulate; a man's man. Yet this same person chooses to defend the existence of fairies, and people have found this difficult. It has been hard for the public to hold in their thoughts both the man who created the ruthless logician Sherlock Holmes; and the man who seeks out photos of goblins from around the world.

I definitely have some questions.

sp: You have not come to your present beliefs lightly, sir.

acd: The subject of psychical research is one upon which I have thought more, and about which I have been slower to form my opinion, than upon any other subject whatever.

sp: And you have not always believed the things you believe today?

acd: No, when I had finished my medical education in 1882, I found myself, like many young medical men, a convinced materialist as regards our personal destiny. I had never ceased to be an earnest theist, because it seemed to me that Napoleon's question to the atheistic professors on the starry night as he voyaged to Egypt: 'Who was it, gentlemen, who made these stars?' – has never been answered. To say that the Universe was made by immutable laws, only put the question one degree further back as to who made the laws. I did not, of course, believe in an anthropomorphic God, but I believed then, as I believe now, in an intelligent force behind all the operations of nature – a force so infinitely complex and great that my finite brain could get no further than its existence. But when it came to a question of our little personalities surviving death, it seemed to me that the whole analogy of nature was against it. This was my frame of mind when spiritual phenomena first came to my notice.

SP: But unlike many, you were at least open to the possibility.

ACD: The day a man's mind shuts is the day of his mental death.

SP: And things changed, because now you believe in ghosts. So tell me – what are they still doing here on earth?

ACD: There is some evidence, which could be cited in full if it did not lead us down a lengthy side street, that when a life has been cut short before it has reached its God-appointed term, whether the cause be murder or suicide – of accident I speak with less confidence – there remains a store of unused vitality which may, where the circumstances are favourable, work itself off in capricious and irregular ways.

SP: A ghost is a life force not yet spent.

ACD: This is, I admit, a provisional theory, but it has been forced upon my mind by many considerations. Such a theory would go some way to explain, or at least to throw some dim light upon, the disturbances which from past time have been associated with scenes of violence and murder. If it could be conceived that the unseen part of a man is divisible into the higher, which passes on as spirit, and the lower, which represents animal functions and mere unused vitality, then it is this latter which has not been normally worked off in a life prematurely ended; and which may express itself in strange semi-intelligent fashion afterwards.

SP: So the ghost is the lower part, left behind on earth, while the higher part travels on.

ACD: It is not a subject upon which one could be dogmatic, but the days are passing when all such cases can be disposed of by being brushed aside and ignored as senseless superstition.

SP: Its not easy territory for those who like rational explanations.

ACD: Perhaps we lose time in searching for rational explanations, since there is ample evidence that there can be rowdiness and hooliganism beyond the veil as well as here!

SP: And so to the fairies.

I expect a little hesitation from the great man; but there is none.

ACD: Fairy and phantom phenomena have been endorsed by so many ages, and even in these material days, seem to break into some lives in the most unexpected fashion.

SP: Not according to the scientists.

ACD: Victorian science would have left the world hard and clean and bare, like a landscape in the moon; but this science is in truth but a little light in the darkness; and outside that limited circle of definite knowledge, we see the loom and shadow of gigantic and fantastic possibilities around us, throwing themselves continually across our consciousness in such ways that it is difficult to ignore them.

SP: You mean fairies?

ACD: Hear this from a lady with whom I have corresponded, who is engaged in organizing work of the most responsible kind: 'My only sight of a fairy,' she says, 'was in a large wood in West Sussex about nine years ago. He was a little creature about half a foot high dressed in leaves. The remarkable thing about his face was that no soul looked through his eyes. He was playing about in long grass and flowers in an open space.'

SP: That is just one testimony; and hardly decisive.

ACD: One of the most gifted clairvoyants in England was the late Mr. Turvey of Bournemouth, whose book, *The Beginnings of Seership*, should be in the library of every student. Mr. Lonsdale of Bournemouth is also a well-known sensitive. The latter has given me the following account of an incident which he observed some years ago in the presence of Mr. Turvey.

'I was sitting,' says Mr. Lonsdale, 'in his company in his garden at Branksome Park. We sat in a hut which had an open front looking on to the lawn. We had been perfectly quiet for some time, neither talking nor moving, as was often our habit. Suddenly I was conscious of a movement on the edge of the lawn, which on that side went up to a grove of pine trees. Looking closely, I saw several little figures dressed in brown peering through the bushes. They remained quiet for a few minutes, and then disappeared. In a few seconds a dozen or more small people about two feet in height, in bright clothes and with radiant faces, ran on to the lawn, dancing hither and thither. I glanced at Turvey to see if he saw anything and whispered, 'Do you see them?' He nodded. These fairies played about, gradually approaching the hut. One little fellow, bolder than the others, came to a croquet hoop close to the hut, and using the hoop as a horizontal bar, turned round and round it, much to our amusement. Some of the others watched him, while others danced about, not in any set dance, but seemingly moving in sheer joy. This continued for four or five minutes, when suddenly, evidently in response to some signal or warning from those dressed in brown, who had remained at the edge of the wood, they all ran into the wood. Just then a maid appeared coming from the house with tea. Never was tea so unwelcome, as evidently its appearance was the cause of the disappearance of our little visitors.'

SP: Frustrating.

ACD: Mr. Lonsdale adds, 'I have seen fairies several times in the New Forest, but never so clearly as this.'

SP: Is Mr Lonsdale of sound mind?

ACD: Knowing Mr. Lonsdale as I do to be a responsible, well-balanced and honourable man, I find such evidence as this very hard to put to one side. Here, at least, the sunstroke hypothesis is negated since both men sat in the shade of the hut and each corroborated the observation of the other. On the other hand, each of the men, like Mrs. Tweedale, was supernormal in psychic development, so that it might well happen that the maid, for example, would not have seen the fairies, even if she had arrived earlier upon the scene.

SP: So these two had special psychic powers? For some, that's a nice way of saying 'deluded'.

ACD: It is easy, of course – for us who only respond to the more material vibrations – to declare that all these seers are self-deluded or are the victims of some mental twist. It is difficult for them to defend themselves from such a charge.

SP: Granted.

ACD: It is, however, to be urged upon the other side that these numerous testimonies come from people who are very solid, practical and successful in the affairs of life. One is a distinguished writer, another an ophthalmic authority, a third a successful professional man, a fourth a lady engaged on public service, and so on. To wave aside the evidence of such people on the ground that it does not correspond with our own experience, is an act of mental arrogance which no wise man will commit.

SP: And while we are with the improbable, there are also stories about stones being moved.

ACD: Numerous. I have particulars of a case in West Sussex which is analogous, and which I have been able to trace to the very lady to whom it happened. This lady desired to make a rock garden, and for this purpose got some large boulders from a field nearby, which had always been known as the pixie stones, and built them into her new rockery. One summer evening this lady saw a tiny grey woman sitting on one of the boulders. The little creature slipped away when she knew that she had been observed. Several times she appeared upon the stones. Later the people in the village asked if the stones might be moved back to the field, 'as,' they said, 'they are the pixie stones and if they are moved from their place, misfortune will happen in the village.' The stones were restored.

SP: And then, of course, there are the famous Cottingley photos – photos taken by two young girls in Yorkshire, which show goblins and elves at play in their garden. And since then, photos of fairies appear to have become quite an industry!

ACD: Yes, all these evidences as to fairies sink into insignificance compared with the actual photographs which I have published in my book *Coming of the Fairies*. These cover cases from Yorkshire, Devonshire, Canada and Germany, and show varying sizes as already described. Since its publication I have had an excellent one from Sweden. They are not all supported by the same degree of evidence, but each case is strong, and all the cases taken together seem to me to be final – unless we are to reconsider altogether our views as to the nature and power of thought-forms.

SP: The authenticity of the Cottingley photos has been seriously questioned.

ACD: No criticism has for a moment shaken the truth of the original Cottingley pictures. All fresh evidence has tended to confirm it.

SP: You had negatives tested at the Kodak works, but they refused to authenticate them. They said there was no evidence of them having been tampered with; but acknowledged there were ways they could have been.

ACD: I was prepared to consider any explanation of these results, save only one which attacked the character of the children.

SP: And you were quite certain that such a trick could not be engineered by two working class girls from Yorkshire – despite the tidal wave of scepticism.

ACD: All nonsense. It seemed to me that those wise entities who were conducting this campaign from the other side, and using some of us as humble instruments, had recoiled before that sullen stupidity against which Goethe said even the Gods themselves fight in vain; and had opened up instead an entirely new line of advance, which will turn that so called 'religious' and essentially irreligious position, which has helped bar our way.

SP: So the gods are allowing sightings of fairies as a sign.

ACD: We had had continued messages at séances for some time that a visible sign was coming through. And perhaps this was what was meant.

sp: OK, but you're a scientific man, Sir Arthur. You like rational explanations. So how do you explain fairies? I have heard you say that they might be like amphibians who live unknown in deep waters, and then one day are seen sunning themselves on a sand bank, before returning to the unseen deeps once more. In the same way, perhaps there's a water's edge in our psyche, above which they sometimes appear.

ACD: Taking the vibration theory as a working hypothesis, one could conceive that by reusing or lowering the rate, the creatures could move from one side to the other of this line of material visibility, as the tortoise moves from the water to the land. This, of course, is supposition; but intelligent supposition based on the available evidence is the pioneer of science; and it may be that the actual solution will be found in this direction.

sp: With reference to the Cottingley photos, a writer in the *Spectator* magazine said, 'One must freely admit that the children who could produce such fakes must be very remarkable children; but then the world, in point of fact, is full not only of very, but very very remarkable children.'

ACD: As I say, I was prepared to consider any explanation of these results, save only one which attacked the character of the children.

sp: But in a way, Sir Arthur, a broader question presents itself here, and it's this: why do fairies matter so much? You have paid a high price in ridicule for your belief in them, perhaps losing more followers than you've gained. Are they so worthy of your attention, when in truth, it's the fate of the human soul which most concerns you? Where's the connection?

ACD: The connection is slight and indirect, consisting only in the fact that anything which widens our conceptions of the possible, and shakes us out of our time-rutted lines of thought, helps us to regain our elasticity of mind and thus to be more open to new philosophies. They can't destroy fairies by antediluvian texts, and when once fairies are admitted, other psychic phenomena will find more ready acceptance.

SP: 'If fairies are possible, then anything is possible'.

ACD: The fairy question is infinitely small and unimportant compared to the question of our own fate and that of the whole human race. The evidence also is very much less impressive; though as I trust I have shown, it is not entirely negligible.

SP: You do almost begin to sound embarrassed about the whole affair.

ACD: It is at the lowest, an interesting speculation which gives an added charm to the silence of the woods and the wildness of the moor land.

TEN

Insufferable Suffragettes and Blind George

In his novella A Duet, *Doyle surely describes a fantasy of himself when he tells us about Frank Crosse. 'There was sometimes just the touch of the savage in Frank Crosse. His intense love of the open air and of physical exercise was a sign of it. He left upon women the impression, not altogether unwelcome, that there were unexplored recesses of his nature to which the most intimate of them had never penetrated. In those dark corners of the spirit either a saint or sinner might be lurking, and there was a pleasurable excitement in peering into them, and wondering which it was. No woman ever found him dull.'*

But some do find Doyle offensive. He detests the suffragette movement; he calls them 'wild women'. He takes particular exception to their violent protests, and feels it is not only pointless for women to have the vote, but unwomanly. The suffragettes have recently responded by putting a dangerous sulphate called vitriol through Doyle's letter box, here at Windlesham.

If the suffragettes bring out the sinner in those dark corners, then perhaps George Edalji brought out the saint. But first, the insufferable suffragettes.

SP: You are forward thinking in many ways; but perhaps not with regard to women; and in particular, Emily Pankhurst.

ACD: Mrs Pankhurst has not a friend in the civilized world.

SP: I think she has quite a few.

ACD: One would think she had been bribed to do these things.

SP: You usually take pleasure in debunking tradition; but in your attitudes to women and the vote, you seem to cling to it.

ACD: The suffragettes are but a small part of London, but their proceedings are so mad that they get into the papers and by that way, the impression goes all over the world.

SP: They pull stunts on behalf of the cause; in the same way that spiritualists do.

ACD: Thus far, public opinion, which usually guides the government in England, has not demanded the entire suppression of the militant suffragette. It has almost come to that stage now, however, and something will happen and happen soon.

SP: What sort of something?

ACD: There will be a wholesale lynching, I fancy, for the English mob, when thoroughly aroused, is not a respecter of sex. If anything happens, the militants will only have themselves to blame. Is that all?

SP: George Edalji.

He is stirred up, and I don't wish to lose him quite yet.

ACD: Yes?

SP: You believed he was falsely convicted; and you yourself became the detective in order to clear him.

ACD: That's right.

SP: You went to meet him, and knew instantly he was innocent of all charges.

ACD: I had been delayed, and he was passing the time reading the paper. He held the paper close to his eyes and rather sideways, proving not only a high degree of myopia, but marked astigmatism. The idea of such a man scouring the fields at night and assaulting cattle, while avoiding the watching police, was ridiculous to anyone who can imagine what the world looks like to eyes with myopia of eight dioptres.

SP: He was accused of night time attacks on cattle?

ACD: Yes. And as I read of the case, the unmistakeable accent of truth forced itself upon my attention and I realized that I was in the presence of an appalling tragedy; and that I was called upon to do what I could do, to set it right.

SP: And in setting it right, you used your medical training; in particular, your study of the eye in Vienna, when still a doctor.

ACD: There in that single physical defect lay the certainty of his innocence.

SP: Indeed, yet it wasn't a happy ending, was it? Because in the end, despite all the evidence, George Edalji was only half-cleared? The police closed ranks; officialdom closed ranks.

ACD: What confronts you is a determination to admit nothing which inculpates another official; and as to the idea of punishing another official for offences which have caused misery to helpless victims, it never comes within their horizons.

SP: And briefly, the Oscar Slater case? Another man unjustly condemned, whose cause you took up.

ACD: I saw that the Oscar Slater case was worse than the

Edalji one, and that this unhappy man had in all probability no more to do with the murder for which he had been condemned than I had.

SP: Yet there was only partial success again; he was still eighteen years behind bars before release. And even though you fought for him, I'm told you did not get on personally.

Doyle shakes his head wearily.

SP: And when on his release he refused to use some of his compensation to pay individuals who had helped him, I believe you wrote to him?

ACD: I did.

SP: What did you say?

ACD: I simply said, 'If you are indeed quite responsible for your actions, then you are the most ungrateful as well as the most foolish person who I have ever known.'

SP: I think we'll move on.

ELEVEN

Passing through the veil

SP: Today, Sir Arthur, you are perhaps the most famous face of the spiritualist movement. But at one time, you looked down on it.

ACD: When I regarded Spiritualism as a vulgar delusion of the uneducated, I could afford to look down upon it; but when it was endorsed by men like Crookes, whom I knew to be the most rising British chemist; by Wallace, who was the rival of Darwin and by Flammarion, the best known of astronomers, I could not afford to dismiss it. It was all very well to throw down the books of these men which contained their mature conclusions and careful investigations, and to say 'Well, he has one weak spot in his brain'; but a man has to be very self-satisfied if the day does not come when he wonders if the weak spot is not in his own brain.

SP: You did, however, have some bad experiences of mediums early on. And even when you trusted the mediums, the messages from the dead seemed rather, well, vacuous. What helped you through?

ACD: I was in practice in Southsea at this time, and dwelling there was General Drayson, a man of very remarkable character, and one of the pioneers of spiritualism in this country. To him I went with my difficulties, and he listened to them very patiently.

SP: And did he have helpful words to say.

ACD: He made light of my criticism of the foolish nature of many of these messages, and of the absolute falseness of some. 'You have not got the fundamental truth into your head,' said he.

SP: And what was that truth?

ACD: 'That truth is,' he said, 'that every spirit in the flesh passes over to the next world exactly as it is, with no change whatever!'

SP: I see. The normal presumption is that someone speaking from beyond the grave is telling the truth; but General Drayson was saying this isn't necessarily so.

ACD: 'This world is full of weak or foolish people,' he said. 'So is the next. You need not mix with them, any more than you do in this world. One chooses one's companions. But suppose a man in this world, who had lived in his house alone and never mixed with his fellows, was at last to put his head out of the window to see what sort of place it was, what would happen? Some naughty boy would probably say something rude. Anyhow, he would see nothing of the wisdom or greatness of the world. He would draw his head in, thinking it was a very poor place. That is just what you have done, Arthur. In a mixed séance, with no definite aim, you have thrust your head into the next world and you have met some naughty boys. Go forward and try to reach something better, my friend.' That was General Drayson's explanation, and though it did not satisfy me at the time, I think now that it was a rough approximation to the truth.

SP: So spirits can lie?

ACD: You may have wildly false messages suddenly interpolated among truthful ones – messages so detailed in their mendacity that it is impossible to think that they are not deliberately false. When once we have accepted the central fact that spirits change little in essentials when leaving the body;

and that in consequence the world is infested by many low and mischievous types, one can understand that these untoward incidents are rather a confirmation of spiritualism than an argument against it.

SP: Fake money wouldn't exist unless there was real money?

ACD: Personally, I have received and have been deceived by, several such messages. I know that I am like a child wading ankle deep in the margin of an illimitable ocean. But this, at least, I have very clearly realized – that the ocean is there.

SP: And of course Holmes admits the possibility of the after-life, does he not, in *The Adventure of the Veiled Lodger*. Could you read Watson's description of the scene?

ACD: 'Then Holmes stretched out his long arm and patted her hand with such a show of sympathy as I had seldom seen him exhibit.

'Poor girl,' he said, 'Poor girl! The ways of fate are indeed hard to understand. If there is not some compensation hereafter, then the world is a cruel jest.'

SP: So you grew slowly into a belief of life after death. And perhaps one landmark moment was the publication in 1903 of a book by Myers, *Human personality and its survival of bodily death*. This excited you.

ACD: It was a great root book from which a tree of knowledge will grow.

SP: It claims – and produces much evidence – that the conscious self is merely the outer garment of a larger, unseen self which is connected to the super-consciousness of the universe. Such a claim clearly gives great support to both mediumship and telepathy.

ACD: The book was an enormous advance. If mind could act on a mind at a distance, then there were some human powers which were quite different to matter as we had always understood it. The ground was cut from beneath the feet of the materialists, and my old position had been destroyed. If the mind, the spirit, the intelligence of man could operate at a distance from the body, then it was a thing to that extent separate from the body. Why should it not exist on its own when the body was destroyed?

SP: And of course since then, you've accumulated vast amounts of material which purports to be messages from those who have passed beyond the veil, reporting back on what it's like.

ACD: I have countless descriptions.

SP: One thing that strikes me after viewing some of them is that they all appear to describe a place quite like earth. And that makes some people suspicious of their authenticity.

ACD: I am aware of all the difficulties connected with such a view of the beyond. We are faced with the obvious reflection that hills and valleys are the result of geological action, of rain and age-long denudation, so that their existence, from our point of view, would seem to imply similar actions in their formation.

SP: That's right.

ACD: Well, it is a legitimate and cogent objection. And yet, the positive agreement of a great number of witnesses cannot be easily set aside. Some have thought that this old earth may have its own etheric body, even as its inhabitants have.

Certainly, if we were to cut out all effects of earthly elemental action, heaven would become a flat and waterless expanse, which would seem more logical than attractive.

SP: But of course your belief in the after life became more than an intellectual enquiry. It came to have a moral force.

ACD: With the actual certainty of a definite life after death, and a sure sense of responsibility for our own spiritual development – a responsibility which cannot be put upon any other shoulders, however exalted, but must be borne by each individual for himself – there will come the greatest reinforcement of morality which the human race has ever known.

SP: You think this will happen?

ACD: We are on the verge of it now, but our descendants will look upon the past century as the culmination of the dark ages when man lost his trust in God, and was so engrossed in his temporary earth life that he lost all sense of spiritual reality.

SP: So tell us clearly – what happens when we die?

ACD: Death makes no abrupt change in the process of development; nor does it make an impassable chasm between those who are on either side of it. No trait of the form and no peculiarity of the mind are changed by death, but all are continued in the spiritual body, which is the counter part of the earthly one at its best, and still contains that core of the spirit which is the very essence of man. Nature develops slowly and not by enormous leaps, so it would seem natural that the soul should not suddenly become devil or angel, but should continue upon its slow growth.

SP: So in physical death, our core spirit of goodness becomes freer to develop?

ACD: The physical basis of all psychic belief is that the soul
is a complete duplicate of the body, resembling it in the
smallest particular, although constructed in some far more
tenuous material. In ordinary conditions, these two bodies are
intermingled so that the identity of the finer one is entirely
obscured. At death, however, and under certain conditions in
the course of life, the two divide and can be seen separately.
Death differs from the conditions of separation before death,
in that there is a complete break between the two bodies, and
life is carried on entirely by the lighter of the two; while the
heavier, like a cocoon from which the living occupant has
escaped, degenerates and disappears, the world burying the
cocoon with much solemnity by taking little pains to ascertain
what has become of its nobler contents.

SP: It sounds like a butterfly emerging from the chrysalis.

ACD: In a painless and natural process the lighter disengages
itself from the heavier, and slowly draws itself off until it
stands with the same mind, the same emotions, and an exactly
similar body, beside the couch of death, aware of those around
and yet unable to make them aware of it – save where that
finer spiritual eyesight called clairvoyance exists.

SP: And is the after-life an enjoyable place? Some people have
a rather drab picture of eternity. The Christian church has
never really succeeded in making it sound interesting.

ACD: In its larger issues, this happy life to come consists in
the development of those gifts which we possess. There is
action for the man of action, intellectual work for the thinker;
artistic, literary, dramatic and religious for those whose God-
given powers lay that way. What we have both in brain and
character we carry over with us. No man is too old to learn,

for what he learns he keeps. There is no physical side to love and no childbirth, though there is close union between those married people who really love each other; and, generally, there is deep sympathetic friendship and comradeship between the sexes.

SP: Jesus said there's no marriage in heaven; but presumably you'd say that doesn't mean there can't be friendships.

ACD: Every man or woman finds a soul mate sooner or later.

SP: And children who died?

ACD: The child grows up to the normal, so that the mother who lost a babe of two years old, and dies herself twenty years later finds a grown-up daughter of twenty-two awaiting her coming. Age, which is produced chiefly by the mechanical presence of lime in our arteries, disappears, and the individual reverts to the full normal growth and appearance of completed man or womanhood. Let no woman mourn her lost beauty, and no man his lost strength or weakening brain. It all awaits them once more upon the other side. Nor is any deformity or bodily weakness there, for all is normal and at its best.

SP: So all is well for the human body and spirit. What about the scenery? Oh, and the climate?

ACD: Happy circles live in pleasant homesteads with every amenity of beauty and of music. Beautiful gardens, lovely flowers, green woods, pleasant lakes, domestic pets – all of these things are fully described in the messages of the pioneer travellers who have at last got news back to those who loiter in the old dingy home. There are no poor and no rich. The craftsman may still pursue his craft, but he does it for the joy of his work. Each serves the community as best he can, while from above come higher ministers of grace, the 'Angels' of holy writ, to direct and help. Above all, shedding down his atmosphere upon all, broods that great Christ spirit, the very soul of reason, of justice and of sympathetic understanding, who has the earth sphere, with all its circles, under his very special care. It is a place of joy and laughter. There are games and sports of all sorts, though none which cause pain to lower life. Food and drink in the grosser sense do not exist; but there seem to be pleasures of taste.

SP: Isn't this picture of heaven just Sir Arthur's wishful thinking?

ACD: I would answer that it is my own conclusion as gathered from a very large amount of existing testimony, and that in its main lines, it has for many years been accepted by those great numbers of silent workers all over the world, who look upon this matter from a strictly religious point of view.

SP: And yet it is not a view that prevails yet.

ACD: Ruskin, an agile mind, said that his assurance of immortality depended upon the observed facts of spiritualism.

SP: Such celebrity support must be helpful.

ACD: Scores, and indeed hundreds, of famous names could be quoted who have subscribed to the same statement, and whose support would dignify any cause upon earth. They are the higher peaks who have been the first to catch the light; but the dawn will spread until none are too lowly to share it.

TWELVE

No place for heroes

I have asked Sir Arthur to write down on a piece of paper the names of three heroes of his. I always think you learn a lot about people from knowing who their heroes are. I have to say the first name on his list is not familiar to me.

SP: The first name in your list of heroes is Daniel Dunglas Home. Why him?

ACD: He was a medium – the greatest on the physical side that the modern world has ever seen.

SP: And clearly a man of outstanding quality in your eyes?

ACD: A lesser man might have used his extraordinary powers to found some special sect of which he would have been the undisputed high priest, or to surround himself with the glamour of power and mystery. Certainly most people in his position would have been tempted to use them for the making of money. As to this latter point, let it be said at once that never in the course of the thirty years of his strange ministry did he touch one shilling as payment for his gifts.

SP: Well, that is remarkable in itself.

ACD: But there are more subtle temptations than those of wealth, and Home's uncompromising honesty was the best safeguard against those. Never for a moment did he lose his humility and his sense of proportion. 'I have these powers,' he would say: 'I shall be happy up to the limit of my strength to demonstrate them to you, if you approach me as one gentleman should approach another. I shall be glad if you can throw any further light upon them. I will lend myself to any reasonable experiment. I have no control over them – they use me, but I do not use them. They desert me for months and then come back in redoubled force. I am a passive instrument – no more.'

SP: Well, he's not getting carried away by himself!

ACD: Such was his unvarying attitude. He was always the easy, amiable man of the world, with nothing either of the mantle of the prophet or of the skullcap of the magician. Like most truly great men, there was no touch of pose in his nature.

SP: So what powers did he display?

ACD: Take this question of levitation as a test of Home's powers. It is claimed that more than a hundred times in good light, before reputable witnesses, he floated in the air. And in these days, when the facts of psychic phenomena are familiar to all, save those who are wilfully ignorant, we can hardly realize the moral courage which was needed by Home in putting forward his powers and upholding them in public.

SP: Why?

ACD: To the average educated Briton in the material Victorian era, a man who claimed to be able to produce results which upset Newton's law of gravity, and which showed invisible mind acting upon visible matter, was prima facie a scoundrel and an impostor.

SP: I see, yes. Vice-Chancellor Gifford was pretty damning.

ACD: The view of spiritualism pronounced by Vice-Chancellor Gifford at the conclusion of the Home-Lyon trial was that of the class to which he belonged.

He knew nothing of the matter, but took it for granted that anything with such claims must be false. No doubt similar things –

SP: – like levitation –

ACD: – No doubt such things were reported in far-off lands and ancient books, but that they could occur in prosaic, steady old England – the England of bank rates and free imports – this was too absurd for serious thought!

SP: So it was found to be impossible because it was thought to be impossible.

ACD: It has been recorded that at this trial Lord Gifford turned to Home's counsel and said, 'Do I understand you to state that your client claims that he has been levitated into the air?' The counsel assented, on which the judge turned to the jury and made such a movement as the high priest may have made in ancient days, when he rent his garments as a protest against blasphemy! In 1867 there were few of the jury who were sufficiently educated to check the judge's remarks, and it is just in that particular that we have made some progress in the fifty years between. Slow work; but Christianity took more than three hundred years to come into its own.

SP: In a court of law, of course, one good witness is sufficient, but your claim is that as far as supernatural powers are concerned, no amount of witnesses is sufficient.

ACD: Indeed. So many are the other instances of Home's levitations, that a long article might easily be written upon this single phase of his mediumship. Professor Crookes was again and again a witness to the phenomenon, and refers to fifty instances which had come within his knowledge. But is there any fair-minded person, who has read the little that I have recorded above, who will not say with Professor Challis, 'Either the facts must be admitted – or the possibility of certifying facts by human testimony must be given up'?

SP: A powerful observation.

ACD: The facts of Home's life are, in my judgment, ample proof of the truth of the spiritualist position, if no other proof at all had been available. It is to be remarked in the career of this entirely honest medium that he had periods in his life when his powers deserted him completely; that he could foresee these lapses, and that, being honest, he simply abstained from all attempts until the power returned.

SP: The power came and went without reason.

ACD: And it is this intermittent character of the gift which is, in my opinion, responsible for cases when a medium who has passed the most rigid tests upon certain occasions, is afterwards detected in simulating, very clumsily, the results which he had once successfully accomplished. The real power having failed, he has not the moral courage to admit it, nor the self-denial to forego his fee – which he endeavours to earn by a travesty of what was once genuine.

SP: But with Home, it sounds like we're back into the age of miracles!

ACD: There is no miracle.

SP: How do you mean? You've just described one with the levitation.

ACD: Nothing on this plane is supernatural. What we see now and what we have read of in ages past, are but the operation of law which has not yet been studied and defined. Already we realize something of its possibilities and of its limitations, which are as exact in their way as those of any purely physical power.

SP: So there is no miracle; just the outworking of natural law. And Home's levitation is part of that.

ACD: We must hold the balance between those who would believe nothing and those who would believe too much. Gradually the mists will clear and we will chart the shadowy coast. When the needle first sprang up at the magnet, it was not an infraction of the laws of gravity. It was that there had been the local intervention of another, stronger force. Such is the case, also, when psychic powers act upon the plane of matter. Had Home's faith in this power faltered, or had his circle been unduly disturbed, he would have fallen. When Peter lost faith, he sank into the waves. Across the centuries the same cause still produced the same effect. Spiritual power is ever with us, if we do not avert our faces; and nothing has been vouchsafed to Judea which is withheld from England.

SP: A good thought. Now to the second name on your list, who is the 18th century figure Emanuel Swedenborg.

ACD: That's right.

SP: Jorge Luis Borges called him the most extraordinary man who ever lived; and many believe he was the true father of spiritualism.

ACD: I agree. His name must live eternally as the first of all modern men who has given a description of the process of death, and of the world beyond, which is not founded upon the vague ecstatic and impossible visions of the old churches, but which actually corresponds with the descriptions which we ourselves obtain from those who endeavour to convey back to us some clear idea of their new existence.

SP: And Jesus Christ is the third name – surprising perhaps, in that you don't care much for his church!

ACD: Christ is the highest spirit known, the Son of God, as we all are – but nearer to God, and therefore in a more particular sense, his son. He does not, save in most rare and special cases, meet us when we die. Since souls pass over, night and day, at the rate of about 100 a minute, this would seem self-evident.

SP: Will we ever see him?

ACD: After a time we may be admitted to his presence, to find a most tender, sympathetic and helpful comrade and guide, whose spirit influences all things – even when his bodily presence is not visible. This is the general teaching of the other world communications concerning Christ; the gentle, loving and powerful spirit which broods ever over that world which, in all its many spheres, is his special care.

SP: So you've spoken of your heroes, Sir Arthur, and attitudes you admire in Home, Swedenborg and Christ. But may I close this particular conversation with the question: which attitudes do you *least* admire?

ACD: The commonest failing, the one which fills the spiritual hospitals of the other world – and is a temporary bar to the normal happiness of the after-life – is the sin of Tomlinson in Kipling's poem; the commonest of all sins in respectable British circles.

SP: And what is that?

ACD: The sin of conventionality, of want of conscious effort and development; of a sluggish spirituality, fatted over by a complacent mind and by the comforts of life. It is the man who is satisfied, the man who refers his salvation to some church or higher power without steady travail of his own soul, who is in deadly danger. All churches are good, Christian or non-Christian, so long as they promote the actual spirit life of the individual. But all are noxious the instant that they allow him to think that by any form of ceremony, or by any fashion of creed, he obtains the least advantage over his neighbour; or can in any way dispense with that personal effort which is the only road to the higher places.

sp: And this challenge is presumably applicable to all?

acd: This is as applicable to believers in spiritualism as to any other belief. If it does not show in practice, then it is vain. One can get through this life very comfortably following without question in some procession with a venerable leader. But one does not die in a procession. One dies alone.

THIRTEEN

The people ask for signs

SP: Though some accuse you of being credulous, Sir Arthur, you are not a man of blind faith.

ACD: 'I never guess. It is a capital mistake to theorize before one has data. Insensibly one begins to twist facts to suit theories, instead of theories to suit facts.'

SP: Sherlock Holmes to Watson, I believe?! In *The Sign of Four*.

ACD: Elementary, my dear Simon!

SP: Well, thank you but I do know that facts have always mattered to you. You started life as a medical man, examining and diagnosing. And the scientist in you has always remained; the scientist who wants evidence and proof. Signs, even.

ACD: We require signs that we can test, before we accept assertions that we cannot test. In the old days, they demanded a sign from the prophet. It was a perfectly reasonable request, and still holds good.

SP: So you required signs of spiritualism. Though I have to say, many of the so-called signs we read in the gutter press, seem rather childish.

ACD: The telephone bell is in itself a very childish affair, but it may be the signal for a very vital message.

SP: That's how you understand the strange occurrences we read about.

ACD: It seemed that all these phenomena, large and small, had been the telephone bells which, senseless in themselves, had signalled to the human race: 'Rouse yourselves! Stand by! Be at attention! Here are signs for you. They will lead up to the message which God wishes to send.' It was the message not the signs that really counted.

SP: So in the time allowed to us this morning, I want to hear of some of the particular signs that aroused you.

ACD: I had a friend who lived in a century-old house and his wife was a sensitive.

SP: A sensitive is someone with particular psychic awareness?

ACD: That's right. And she was continually aware of a distinct push when she came down the stairs, always occurring upon the same step.

SP: Dangerous, unless you're ready for it.

ACD: Well, afterwards it was discovered that an old lady who had formerly lived in the house received a playful push from some frolicsome child, and lost her balance, falling down the stairs.

SP: So what did you make of that?

ACD: It is not necessary to believe that some hob goblin lingered upon that stair continually repeating the fatal action.

SP: Maybe not; though it's a rather nice image!

ACD: The probable explanation seems to be that the startled mind of the old woman as she felt herself falling, left some permanent effect behind it which could still be discerned in this strange fashion.

SP: But on what could an impression be left?

ACD: An impression of such a nature becomes a material thing and implies a material nexus, however subtle.

SP: Something physical on which an imprint can be made?

ACD: So far as we know there are only two things there, the air and the ether. The air is a mobile thing and could not carry a permanent impression. But is the ether a mobile thing? It is pictured as a most delicate medium with vibrating currents flowing in it, but it seems to me that a most tenuous jelly with quivers and thrills would be a closer analogy. We could conceive the whole material universe embedded in and interpenetrated by this subtle material, which would not necessarily change its position since it is too fine for wind or any coarser material to influence it.

SP: That's quite a proposal.

ACD: I feel that I am rushing in, yes, but if it should prove to be as I suggest then we should have that permanent screen on which shadows are thrown. The block of ether upon the stairs is the same that it always was, and so conveys the impression from the past.

SP: And tell me – are you yourself psychic?

ACD: I am by no means psychic myself, and yet I am conscious, quite apart from imagination, of a curious effect, almost a darkening of the landscape with a marked sense of heaviness, when I am on an old battlefield.

SP: You sense the struggle and the pain?

ACD: I have been particularly conscious of it on the scenes of Hastings and Culloden, two fights where great causes were finally destroyed and where extreme bitterness may well have filled the hearts of the conquered. The shadow still remains. A more familiar example of the same faculty is the gloom which gathers over the mind of even an average person upon entering certain houses.

SP: A stately home had that effect on me.

ACD: The most rabid agitator need not envy our nobility their stately old castles, for it is happier to spend one's life in the simplest cottage, uncontaminated by psychic disturbance, than to live in the grandest mansion which still preserves the gloomy taints that hang about rooms once perhaps the scene of cruelty or other vices.

SP: You have, over the years, gathered many people's stories of strange events and of signs.

ACD: One correspondent lived in an old house in the West End of London. It was a winter night, and she was lying half asleep when she heard a sound as of the crackling of parchment, and opening her eyes, she saw a man seated in a chair in front of the fire.

SP: What sort of man?

ACD: He was dressed in a uniform reminiscent of Nelson's days, with brass buttons, wore powdered hair with a black bow, and was staring rigidly into the glow, while he held crumpled up in his right hand some sort of document. He was a stately and handsome figure. For some hours he sat there, the fire gleaming, when it spurted up upon the buckles and buttons of his dress. Finally, in the small hours of the morning, he vanished gradually away.

sp: So what happened?

acd: Several times later the lady saw the same apparition, and it might well be argued that it was constantly there, but that its perception depended upon the condition of the clairvoyant. Finally, I believe some religious exorcism was performed in the room and the vision was not seen again.

sp: So what do you deduce, Sherlock?

acd: This case clearly fits itself into the hypothesis of a form-picture being thrown out at a time of emotion. The parchment document suggests a will or some other paper of importance which the officer has prepared or received, but which in either case, may have caused him so much mental stress as he brooded over it in front of the fire that he threw this permanent record upon the screen of time.

sp: You have another letter in your hand.

acd: This letter takes us back into the black days of the War. It is from an English lady living in Finland. Her younger brother was killed at the front in one of the final battles, in a dawn attack. At that hour, the lady went through his whole experience, visualized the battlefield, heard the guns and saw an elderly and moustached German who threw something – presumably a bomb – which struck her down. Some nights later she had a second equally vivid dream, in which a radiant spirit led her along a poplar-lined French road and halted at last at the spot where the dead body of her brother was lying.

sp: Perhaps her dreams were her dread and expectation that her brother was bound to be killed.

acd: Not at all. She declares that she had every reason at the time to think that her brother was at a depot and not in the firing line. It was only after the Armistice that official news was given of his death. This is one of a class of cases which has been so common that no reasonable man can deny them. To explain them is another matter, for even if one accepts the full faith of spiritualism, there is a good deal which is inexplicable.

SP: Indeed. I mean, who is it that's passing the news to her via the dream? How does it happen? And why? There's a lot that's unexplained.

ACD: The dream which duplicates an actual occurrence is hard to explain, but an even tougher problem is presented by the prophetic dream which gives a picture of the future. A gentleman once dreamed that he saw a lady friend working at some pink material. On inquiry the next day, she said, 'Yes, I stayed up late last night making a crêpe de Chine blouse of pink stuff, which I particularly wished to finish.' Since she was late, it is probable that his dream saw that which was actually occurring at the moment, and that it was an instance of what has been called 'travelling clairvoyance' where the etheric body brings back information – surprisingly trivial information at times – to the unconscious material brain.

SP: So that's an intriguing dream; but not ultimately very important; no one was helped.

ACD: Ah, but they are occasionally of a very helpful character, as the next example will show. The writer is a Manchester man fresh from Cambridge. During a visit to Switzerland he dreamed that he was in a tropical land, sandy, with a shimmering heat and an intensely blue sky. Suddenly, a huge man appeared before him holding a triangular dagger of peculiar shape, with which he made the motion of striking. He then vanished. Next day, the youth explored a disused tunnel. This is his report:

'I went in and found magnificent icicles hanging from the roof. All at once I saw one very large one. It was triangular and came to a sharp point. I thought of my dream, and recognized the triangular dagger. I stopped, and at that moment, the whole thing fell with a crash. It must have weighed at least two hundred pounds and would perhaps have killed me."

SP: I'm wondering if it's just coincidence. And I'm also wondering how you explain the tropical scene.

ACD: I would only suggest – but with all reserve – that many of us believe that we have guides or guardian angels. These guides would appear to be often drawn from the Oriental races. Supposing that this youth's guide was an Egyptian he might, in warning his pupil, have brought back with him some impression of his native land. The student remarked that the dagger was of a shape which was once used in Ancient Egypt. Such an explanation may stand until a better one is found.

SP: Well one thing is sure – psychic investigation is not a dull affair!

ACD: If anyone craves for adventure, he will find it in psychic work. I have myself encountered many incidents in actual fact which I could hardly beat if I gave free play to my imagination.

SP: Better even than your own stories? You mentioned the Wicklands to me in the kitchen.

ACD: Dr. and Mrs. Wickland of Los Angeles have occasionally found their way into the Press. He is a deep student of psychic phenomena believing, as I do myself, that a great deal of mania and crime is due to direct obsession; and that recognition of the fact would be the first necessary step for dealing with it. His wife is a medium who is very sensitive to spirit presences, and is ready, with great bravery, to allow them to control her so long as she thinks a good purpose can be served. She is, in my opinion, one of the heroines of the world.

SP: High praise.

ACD: Such were the couple, gentle, elderly folk, who drove out with us to see something of rural Sussex.

SP: I sense an adventure.

ACD: I took them to the old moated grange of Groombridge, which is mentioned by Evelyn in his diary. As we stood looking at the lichened brick walls, a door which gave upon the deep moat opened, and a woman looked out. Then it closed again. We passed on, and I thought no more of the matter.

SP: But more was to come?

ACD: As we walked through the meadow which led to the high road, Mrs. Wickland kept glancing back. Presently she said:

'There is such a strange old man walking beside us.'

'What is he like?'

'He is old. His face is sunk forward. His back is hunched. He is earth-bound.'

'How is he dressed?'

'He has knee-breeches, a striped vest, and quite a short coat.'

'Whence did he come?'

'He came through that door that opened.'

'Then how did he cross the moat?'

'I don't know, and I don't know what he wants, but he is at our heels.'

SP: So what did you do?

ACD: I took my guests to the old Crown Inn in the village, where we had tea. Mrs. Wickland kept glancing at a chair in the corner beside her.

'He is there,' she said, and presently began to laugh. 'I did not in the least want that second cup of tea, and the extra slice,' she said, 'but he was close to me, and would have taken possession and helped himself if I had not done so.'

SP: Interesting day out.

ACD: We then drove home and were seated among the roses on my veranda, the Wicklands, my wife and myself. We were talking of other things when the Seer suddenly gave a start.

'He's here!'

Then came the amazing moment. Before our eyes, Mrs Wickland changed in an instant into a heavy-faced, sullen old man, with bent back and loose, senile lips.

SP: That's what you saw?

ACD: The whole expression was utterly different. She choked and spluttered in an effort to express the thoughts of the control.

SP: So what did you do?

ACD: Dr. Wickland, with the quiet assurance of long practice, massaged the throat.

'All right, friend, give yourself time.'

The newcomer shook off his hand angrily.

'Leave me alone. What do you want to touch me for?' he croaked.

From that time, the dialogue was as follows, sometimes one and some times another asking the questions, and with occasional gasping and choking as interruption.

'Who are you?'

'I am from Groombridge. My name? Well, I don't feel clear in my mind, yes, yes, I remember. It is David. And Fletcher. That is it, David Fletcher. Yes, I have been in service there. Horses. Yes, it was the horses I looked to. What year is it? I don't know. My mind ain't clear. Is it 1808 or is it 1809? What d'ye say, 1927? Well, well, that's a good 'un.'

'You're dead.'

'Dead, why, I am here talkin' to you. How can I be dead? I'd be with God if I was dead. Look at my hand? Why, there are rings on it. They look like my lady's rings. No, I don't know how they came to be there. I don't understand a lot of things. I don't know who them folk are in the house. They have no call to be there. Me and the others try to put them out.'

('The others,' Dr. Wickland explained, 'were probably other earth-bound spirits in the old house.')

'Yes, master was a good master, but he died, and the others came in. The house was sold. We wasn't well treated after that. What could I do? No, I couldn't go away. Where was I to go out in the wide world, and me with a hump on my back? I belonged to the house. I had to do the best I could. What have I done? I don't rightly understand it. I've slept always in the same old corner. It seems a long, long time.'

'Now tell us, David, don't you remember being very ill?'

'Me ill? No, I was never ill. But I'll tell you what happened. He pushed me into the water.'

'Into the moat?'

'Yes, into the water.'

'Who was he?'

'It was Sam. But I held on to him, I did. He came in the water, too.'

(Dr. Wickland remarked that the man was probably drowned on that occasion.)

'Is there no one who loved you among the dead? Was your mother dead?'

'Mother was dead. No one ever loved me, except mother. She loved me, mother did. No one could love me, because I looked queer. They laughed.'

(He burst into noisy sobbing.) 'Mother loved me. Nobody else. They said it wasn't right that I wait upon the ladies, and me with a hump.'

'Cheer up, David; we will soon get the hump off you. How came you to follow us?'

'I don't know. I think I was told. Then I got bread and tea. I have not had tea since I can remember. I would like more. I am always hungry. But what was that wagon? That was the devil's wagon, I think. I got in, but it went that fast that I was a feared to get out again.' (This was my motor.)

'It's as well for you that you did not, David, for we are going to do you good. First of all, you have got to realize that you are dead. You were drowned that time you fell into the moat.'

'Well I never. That's a queer idea.'

'Now understand this.' (It is Dr. Wickland, who is talking in cool, gentle, assured tones.) 'You can do anything now by the power of thought, if you know how to use it. This hump of yours. Take it off. Take it off, I say. Your back is as straight as mine.'

(The bent figure began to straighten up and to sit erect in the chair. Suddenly both hands were thrown forward.)

'Mother, mother.' (His face had become younger, more intelligent and was shining with ecstasy.) 'I see her and it's mother, but she looks younger than I can remember.'

'She will take charge of you now. You have been brought here by higher powers for a purpose – to save you. Do you want to go back to the old house?'

'No, no, I want to go to mother. Oh, you good kind people' – the rest was just incoherent gratitude.

SP: My goodness!

ACD: And so it was that the earth-bound ostler found his mother at last, among the rambler roses of my balcony. Have I not said truly that the actual experiences of the spiritualist, of which this is one in a hundred, are stranger far than what I should dare to invent?

SP: And of course most will say it is a fairy tale.

ACD: How about the change in the medium? How about the ostler's dress so accurately described? No, it is not a fairy-tale, but a new realm of knowledge which the human race has now to explore and to conquer.

SP: And the purpose of these signs?

ACD: I believe that all these varied experiences have been sent to us, not to amuse us by tales to be told and then forgotten, but as the essential warp and woof of a new spiritual garment which is to be woven for the modern world. We live in an age which has long demanded a sign, yet when the sign was sent it was blind to it. I cannot understand the frame of mind of those who view proofs of survival which appear in the Bible as of most vital importance; and yet close their mind to the same thing when they reappear before our very eyes!

SP: Perhaps it's always true that the prophet is not recognized in his own town. When distant tales are told of him, he sounds intriguing, convincing, noble even. But when he knocks on our own door, we always need more time, more signs, more proof. And for yourself, Sir Arthur, it seems most of the proof has come through others, as opposed to your own direct experiences.

ACD: Apart from the ordinary phenomena of the séance room, my life has not given me much direct psychic experience, no. I have, so far as I know, no spiritual gifts myself and none of that psychic atmosphere which gives a tinge of romance to so many lives.

SP: You sound a bit sad about that.

ACD: There have, however, been occasions when without the aid of a medium, I have been sensitive to the unknown.

SP: An example?

ACD: One instance occurred some years ago, and it was here in my bedroom. I wakened in the night with the clear consciousness that there was someone in the room, and that the presence was not of this world. I was lying with my back to the room, acutely awake, but utterly unable to move. It was physically impossible for me to turn my body and face this visitor. I heard measured steps across the room. I was conscious, without seeing it, that someone was bending over me; and then I heard a voice saying in a loud whisper, 'Doyle, I come to tell you that I am sorry.' A minute later my disability disappeared, and I was able to turn, but all was black darkness and perfectly still. My wife had not awakened, and knew nothing of what had passed.

SP: It was perhaps a dream?

ACD: It was no dream; I was perfectly conscious all the time. My visitor gave no name, but I felt that it was a certain individual to whom I had tried to give psychic consolation when he was bereaved. He rejected my advances with some contempt and died himself shortly afterwards. It may well be that he wished to express regret. As to my own paralysis it came, I have no doubt, from the fact that the power for the manifestation had been drawn out of me.

SP: Jesus talks of the power leaving his body on one occasion;

when someone needs him.

ACD: When spirit manifests upon the physical plane, it has to draw its matter from a material source, and I was the obvious one. It is the one occasion upon which I have been used as a physical medium, and I am content that it should be the last.

SP: And all these signs, Sir Arthur – they are signs pointing to a great discovery; perhaps the greatest discovery?

ACD: All recent discoveries, whether they be of aviation, wireless telegraphy or other material novelties, are insignificant beside a development which shows us a new form of matter, with unheard-of properties, lying latent in all probability within each of us. By a strange paradox, the searchers after spirit have come to know more about matter, and its extraordinary possibilities, than any materialist has learned.

SP: And we haven't yet touched on ectoplasm, to which you attach great importance. A German doctor, Schrenck-Notzing, investigated and wrote about it.

ACD: A single sentence from the preface gives the gist of his book. He says: 'We have very often been able to establish that, by an unknown biological process, there comes from the body of the medium a material, at first semi-fluid, which possesses some of the properties of a living substance – notably that of the power of change, of movement, and of the assumption of definite forms.'

SP: So there's a semi-fluid coming from the body of the medium, which somehow has a life of its own?

ACD: The results are, in my opinion, among the most notable of any investigation which has ever been recorded. It was testified by witnesses, and shown by the photographs, that there oozed from the medium's mucous membranes, and occasionally from her skin, this extraordinary gelatinous material.

SP: I've seen the pictures.

ACD: Well, the pictures are strange and repulsive, but many of nature's processes seem so in our eyes. You can see this streaky, viscous stuff hanging like icicles from the chin, dripping down on to the body and forming a white apron, or projecting in shapeless lumps from the orifices of the face. When touched – or when undue light came upon it – it writhed back into the body as swiftly and stealthily as the tentacles of a hidden octopus. If seized and pinched, the medium cried aloud. It would protrude through clothes and vanish again, leaving hardly any trace upon them. With the assent of the medium, a small piece was amputated.

SP: And what happened?

ACD: It dissolved in the box in which it was placed, as snow would have done, leaving moisture and some large cells which might have come from a fungus.

SP: I can see it is a phenomenon that requires explanation. But what has this to do with the spirit world?

ACD: What follows is far stranger, and will answer that question.

SP: So reveal all. .

ACD: You must know, then, utterly incredible as it may appear, that this substance, after forming, begins in the case of some mediums, to curdle into definite shapes, and those shapes are human limbs and human faces, seen at first in two dimensions upon the flat; and then moulding themselves at the edges until they become detached and complete.

SP: You mean this substance actually turns into people of some sort?

ACD: Very many of the photographs exhibit these strange phantoms, which are often much smaller than life.

SP: I'm intrigued; but still trying to see the link with spiritualism.

ACD: The next stage takes us all the way. When the medium is at her best – and it occurs only at long intervals and at some cost to her own health – there forms a complete figure; and this figure is moulded to resemble some deceased person.

SP: So a deceased person is appearing through the medium's excretions?

ACD: The cord which binds it to the medium is loosened; a personality which either is, or pretends to be, that of the dead takes possession of it, and the breath of life is breathed into the image, so that it moves and talks and expresses the emotions of the spirit within.

SP: Through the medium's ectoplasm, a figure from the past is given new birth.

ACD: The last word of the record is this: 'Since these séances, and on numerous occasions, the entire phantom has shown itself, it has come out of the cabinet, has begun to speak, and has reached Mme Bisson, one of the investigators, whom it has embraced on the cheek. The sound of the kiss was audible.'

SP: The ectoplasm figure kissed the researcher?

ACD: Was there ever a stranger finale of a scientific investigation? It may serve to illustrate how impossible it is for even the cleverest of materialists to find any explanation of such facts which are consistent with his theories.

SP: Some said it was simply food being regurgitated.

ACD: A close-meshed veil was worn over the medium's face in some of the experiments, without in the least hampering the flow of the ectoplasm.

SP: But you can understand scepticism at such amazing occurrences.

ACD: Of course. These results, though checked in all possible ways, were none the less so amazing that the inquirer had a right to suspend judgment until they were confirmed. But this has been fully done. Dr. Schrenck-Notzing returned to Munich and there he was fortunate enough to find another medium, a Polish lady, who possessed the faculty of materialization. He obtained hair from one of the materialized forms, and compared it microscopically with hair from the medium. These tests showed that the hair could not be from the same person.

SP: You mean the hair of the ectoplasm creature was not biologically the same as that of the medium?

ACD: Truly, the story of the Italian Cardinals and Galileo will seem reasonable when compared with the attitude of Victorian science to this invasion of the beyond!

SP: And what about the theologians?

ACD: Of the theologians I say nothing, for that is another aspect of the matter, and they have only lived up to their own record; but material science – which made mock of mesmerism until, for very shame, it had to change its name to hypnotism before acknowledging it – has a sad reckoning before it, in the case of spiritualism. The fear is lest their actions go too far, and in contemplating its colossal blunder, we may forget or underrate the thousand additions which science *has* made to the comfort of the human race.

SP: You don't wish for a back lash against science. If it has been blind to spiritualism, it has seen clearly much else.

ACD: Be that as it may, who can read the facts here quoted and doubt that in those mists and shadows which hang round this uncharted coast, we have at least one solid, clear-cut cape which juts out into the sunshine? Behind, however, lies a hinterland of mystery which successive generations of pioneers will be called upon to explore.

SP: Including spirit photography, which we've already spoken of in relation to the fairies.

ACD: The most successful results are obtained by the Crewe circle in England, under the mediumship of Mr. Hope and Mrs. Buxton. I have seen scores of these photographs, which in several cases reproduce exact images of the dead which do not correspond with any pictures of them taken during life. I have seen father, mother and dead soldier son, all taken together, with the dead son looking far the happier and not the least substantial of the three.

SP: But to repeat myself, spiritualism can seem rather stunt-driven. 'Oh look, a chair that flies!' 'My oh my! A man who rises off the ground!' 'Photos in which the dead appear!' Some will say 'So what?' But you say, 'The signs point to something greater.'

ACD: The exhibition of a force which is beyond human experience and human guidance is but a method of calling attention. To repeat a simile with which I started, it is the humble telephone bell which heralds the all-important message. In the case of Christ, the Sermon on the Mount was worth more than many miracles. In the case of this new development, the messages from beyond are more than any phenomena. A vulgar mind might make Christ's story seem vulgar, if it insisted upon loaves of bread and the bodies of fish. So, also, a vulgar mind may make psychic religion vulgar, by insisting upon moving furniture or tambourines in the air. In each case, they are crude signs of power, and the essence of the matter lies upon higher planes.

SP: Yet you can still see its weaker, or as you say, more vulgar side?

ACD: Of course. I have made this plain. The weaker side of spiritualism lies in the fact that its adherents have largely been drawn from the less educated part of the community.

SP: With what result?

ACD: A presentment of the philosophy which has often repelled earnest minds; and in no way represents its true scope and significance.

SP: So it's been a problem of presentation by the less educated?

ACD: Yes, alongside no systematic cultivation of the gift of mediumship – this also being the fault of the community and the law, with the result that it has often fallen into unworthy hands and been exercised for purely utilitarian and worldly motives.

SP: You mean money.

ACD: A retinue of rogues have been attracted to the movement by the fact that séances have been largely held in the dark, when the object has been to produce physical phenomena. This has served as a screen for villainy and the effect has been increased occasionally by the systematic use of conjuror's apparatus, yes.

SP: So finally, Sir Arthur, in the light of the signs we have discussed: is spiritualism a religion?

ACD: It will end by being the proof and basis of all religions, rather than a religion in itself.

FOURTEEN

Family Fortunes

Sir Arthur Conan Doyle was one of ten children, of whom seven survived. He draws a veil over his father's alcoholism in his memoirs; though he deals with the subject severely in his work. His father died Oct 10th in 1893, in Crighton Royal Institution, Dumfries – the same year they discovered that Touie, his first wife, had tuberculosis. The cause of death was given as 'epilepsy of many years standing'.

Throughout his incarcerations, Charles Doyle kept review copies of all Arthur's books, and held his son in considerable admiration. But Arthur's feelings towards him were mixed, with shame and anger revealed in his fictional work. His story called The Sealed Room, *for instance, involves a father who, unable to pay his debts, locks himself in a sealed room, takes poison and dies there, not wishing to place yet more stress on his wife who has a heart condition. While* The Japanned Box, *another of his tales, features a man who has lived a life of drinking and gambling, sitting by a phonograph several times a day, playing back his dead wife's pleadings not to indulge in the drinking which had ruined him as a young man.*

Here is a world of locked rooms, thick walls and dark secrets; a world where the dead wield power over the living; where advice is tragically unheeded, where alcohol destroys and where pain lives on.

As for Touie, her illness took the family to the dry heat of Egypt in 1896, where the ever-energetic Sir Arthur climbed the Great Pyramid, played golf on the links of the Mena hotel and practiced riding. And the family journey up the Nile led to his novel The Tragedy of Korosko, *in which a group of Moslem fanatics hold captive a group of British tourists.*

He called the birth of Kingsley, their first son, 'the chief event of their life'. Sir Arthur remained celibate during Touie's illness; but fell hopelessly in love with Jean Leckie as soon as he saw her in 1897. She became the most important woman in his life, apart from his mother. Concerning his mother, he maintained the habit of writing to her throughout his life. He started at the age of nine when sent away to Jesuit boarding school.

His family story was soon entwined with his spiritualist practice. He believed he'd experienced the materialized spirit of his mother through the mediums William and Eva Thompson. Within days, they were exposed as frauds and arrested by police at another séance, where they found wigs, costumes and fluorescent make-up. But Sir Arthur was unmoved, publicly at least.

Kingsley himself was wounded at the Somme, and died of pneumonia in London in 1918. But he too was to visit Sir Arthur from beyond the grave.

Doyle had two children with Touie, Kingsley and Mary. As a father, they said that he was a loveable but slightly fearsome character. He could be reckless and boyish with them one moment, but when tired or worried, curt and sharp with them the next. There was clearly much strain at home after 1897, when Doyle met Jean. Some of his friends were critical of his attachment to Jean, and it must have been a confusing time for him – genuine upset at Touie's illness, alongside his obsession with Jean. He escaped into writing, for as Holmes said to Watson: 'Work is the best antidote to sorrow.'

Touie died in 1906, aged 49. And the following year, after nine years of secret courtship, Arthur and Jean married. They moved to Windlesham in Sussex, where he has spent the rest of his life.

I do not expect Sir Arthur to speak of his family; it is complicated on so many levels. But as the light fades on his garden, he insists that we do a little weeding. It is not a wise thing for him to undertake, for he is quickly breathless. But in between the flower bed and the wheel barrow, I do learn a little.

SP: You married Louisa Hawkins, or Touie, in 1885. How would you describe her?

ACD: Gentle and amiable.

SP: And when Touie was diagnosed with 'Galloping consumption' – which we now call tuberculosis, of course – you were shocked into immediate action.

ACD: I set all my energy to work to save the situation. The home was abandoned, the newly brought furniture sold, and we made for Davos in the High Alps where there seemed the best chance of killing this accursed microbe, which was rapidly eating out her vitals. And we succeeded, postponing the fatal issue from 1893 to 1906.

SP: Indeed.

He removes himself to another flower bed. I wonder if I will have more luck asking about his son's post-death appearances.

SP: After the death of your son Kingsley in the Great War, you were eager to establish contact with him through a medium. And one spoke through your son's ring?

ACD: She was able to tell me the initials on the ring of my boy, who died some months before.

SP: This was a ring which you placed in a sealed box; along with other members of the audience seeking news of lost loved ones.

ACD: The average person examining the ring would perhaps have made nothing of it. It was so worn that it would be excusable if you could not make anything of it, even if you had seen it before.

I do not raise the matter, for fear of offence, but a few days after this sitting, the medium's agent confessed that the trick was done by exchanging the box holding the audience items. The medium held a false box, while the real one was examined in an adjoining room; and information about the objects fed through.

SP: And then on another occasion, a certain Mrs B. helped you into contact with your son. What did he say?

ACD: My boy tried to console me at his death and said that in any case, he would have not stayed in England, as he had intended to go abroad in the medical service.

SP: Did he speak of his death?

ACD: He told me that he had suffered pain in his lungs – which was quite true, because he died from pneumonia after serving in the army three years. He referred to other friends who had passed over, and said, 'When I was alive I did not believe in spiritualism. Now I believe in it. I was a chuckle-headed ass not to believe it.'

SP: But this encounter was the prelude to your best meeting with him.

ACD: There came to me what was the supreme moment in my spiritual experience. It is almost too sacred for full description, and yet I feel that God sends such gifts that we might share them with others.

SP: So what happened?

ACD: There came a voice in the darkness, a whispered voice saying, 'Jean, it is I.' My wife felt a hand upon her head, and cried 'It is Kingsley!' I heard the word 'Father'. I said, 'Dear boy, is that you?' I then had a sense of a face very close to my own, and of breathing. Then the clear voice came again with an intensity and note very distinctive of my son, 'Forgive me!' he said. I told him eagerly that I had no grievance of any kind. A large strong hand then rested upon my head, it was gently bent forward, and I felt and heard a kiss just below my brow. 'Tell me dear, are you happy?' I cried. There was silence, and I feared he was gone. Then on a sighing note came the words, 'Yes, I am so happy.'

I ask no more questions about his family. But I do want to leave on record a note he wrote to Jean in 1923, about the children from his second marriage, Denis, Adrian and Jean. She offered it to me today, as we talked in the hall, and I pass it on to you:

'The boys are but shallow sparkling pools compared to this little girl with her self-repression and dainty aloofness. You know the boys; you never feel that you quite know the girl! Something very strong and forceful appears to be at the back of that wee body. Her will is tremendous. Nothing can break or even bend it. The boys are helpless if she has really made up her mind. But this is only when she asserts herself, and those are rare occasions. As a rule, she sits quiet, aloof, affable, keenly alive to all that passes and yet taking no part in it, save for some subtle smile or glance. And then suddenly the wonderful grey-blue eyes under the long black lashes will gleam like coy diamonds, and such a hearty little chuckle will come from her that everyone else is bound to laugh out of sympathy.'

FIFTEEN

End Things

Last year, despite suffering from angina, he undertook a psychic tour of Holland, Denmark Sweden and Norway. On his return, he was so ill he had to be carried ashore, and has been bedridden ever since. I have been told, however, that he has managed one last adventure. Getting out of bed on a cold spring day, unseen, he went downstairs and into the garden. When he was found later, he was lying on the ground, one hand clutching his heart, the other holding a single white snow drop.

SP: You are a fighter to the end, Sir. You are presently doing all in your powers to challenge the Witchcraft Act?

ACD: I am.

SP: Placed on the statute books in the reign of James 1ˢᵗ, the authorities have found it a convenient means of prosecuting mediums.

ACD: We have no desire to uphold cheats or charlatans, but at present the very existence of spiritual powers is in practice denied by the law of England, and the Apostolic circle –

SP: – you mean Jesus' disciples? –

ACD: – yes, they themselves would have been liable to criminal arrest as are our mediums! This is an intolerable situation.

SP: But away from the political struggles, Sir Arthur, this morning you showed me a poem you wrote about yourself. It is called *The Inner Room* and describes your various identities. I wondered if you might read it.

ACD: *The Inner Room* – by myself!

There are others who are sitting
Grim as doom
In the dim ill-boding shadow
Of my room.
Darkling figures, stern or quaint,
Now a savage, now a saint,
Showing fitfully and faint
Through the gloom.
And those shadows are so dense,
There may be
Many – very man – more
Than I see.
They are sitting day and night
Soldier, rogue and anchorite;
And they wrangle and they fight
Over me.

SP: Wonderful; perhaps we all should compose our own version. But I am compelled to change direction once again and ask finally about a recent arrival in your life. Since 1922, a new voice has entered your sphere; that of the Arabian spirit called Pheneas, who has called himself your personal guide.

ACD: Indeed.

SP: He speaks through your wife Jean's automatic writing and trance speaking, describes terrible events to come, and says you have a special task.

ACD: To prepare men's minds, so that when the awakening comes they shall be more ready to receive it.

SP: Now I hope I've got this right, but from what I gather, Pheneas says God's light must descend and burn up the evil flames; that the coming 'world-surrender' to God would start at harvest time in 1925, with a great storm moving from west to east, followed by 'a tremendous upheaval in Central Europe, the submerging of a continent, and then a great light from on high.' I mean, no offence, but this all sounds like the final book in the bible, the apocalyptic Revelation! Here the Vatican is declared a 'sink of iniquity', which will be 'wiped off the face of the globe.' But according to Pheneas, you, Sir Arthur, will be quite safe, for there's a 'power station' being erected around your home, to protect you, as the final battle is fought out.

ACD: The whole process will take some years, but I shall survive to the end, then pass over with my whole family.

SP: A claim which certainly ties in with a medium from Winnipeg who has predicted that you will 'not die in the ordinary sense.' Are you comfortable with such talk?

ACD: The world has failed to learn the lesson of the great war, and only by such tragic visitations can it be chastened and humbled into a more spiritual state of mind, and that accordingly, unless there is some sweeping change of heart, a second trial is coming which will surely accomplish what the first has failed to do. The date of this crisis will be soon; it will take the form of political and natural convulsions, and its effect will be absolutely shattering. Such, in a nutshell, is the message as we have received it.

SP: Not a pleasant message.

ACD: It is not a pleasant one either to hear, or to deliver, at a time when we are still reeling from the last blow, but if the message is a true one then the situation should be faced.

SP: Our time is up, Sir Arthur – perhaps in more ways than one, if what you say is true. But people have asked me to ask these questions, and so I do. Your favourite Sherlock Holmes story?

ACD: *The Speckled Band.*

SP: Your favourite piece of fiction written by you?

ACD: My novel *The White Company.*

SP: And finally, how would you like to be remembered?

ACD: I should dearly love that the world should be ever so little better for my presence. Even on this small stage we have our two sides, and something might be done by throwing all one's weight, breadth, tolerance, charity, temperance, peace and kindliness to man and beast. We can't all strike very big blows; but even the little ones count for something.

SP: 'It has long been an axiom of mine that the little things are infinitely the most important.' Your very own Sherlock Holmes, in *A case of identity.*

ACD: Well, Sherlock is always right!

SP: But in truth, Sir Arthur, spiritualism is the only 'right' for you, is it not?

ACD: True. I'd give family, title, whatever fortune I possess, my literary reputation – they are all as mud in the gutter to what this thing is to me. I know that it explains all of life to me; and I know how inexplicable life was before.

SP: But what a battle it's been!

ACD: We who believe in the psychic revelation, and who appreciate that a perception of these things is of the utmost importance, certainly have hurled ourselves against the obstinacy of our time. Possibly we have allowed some of our lives to be gnawed away in what, for the moment, seems a vain and thankless quest. Only the future can show whether the sacrifice was worth it. Personally I think that it was.

SIXTEEN

Afterword

The medium from Winnipeg was wrong. Conan Doyle did die an ordinary death, if such a thing there is, on July 7th, 1930. His last words before departing for 'the greatest and most glorious adventure of all' were addressed to his wife: 'You are wonderful' he whispered.

At his funeral, the Rev. Thomas read out a statement written by his wife, Lady Conan Doyle:

'We know that it is only the natural body that we are committing to the ground. The etheric body is the exact duplicate, and lives on, and is able when the psychic conditions are attuned to the spiritual, even to show itself to earthly human eyes. The beloved one here will continue to keep in close touch with the family; although they may not have the power to see his presence. Only those who have that God-given extra sight – clairvoyance – will be able actually to see his form. Sir Arthur will continue to carry on the work of telling the world the truth.'

The epitaph on his on his gravestone is this:

Steel True
Blade Straight
Arthur Conan Doyle
Knight
Patriot, Physician and Man of Letters

The End

Simon Parke

Simon Parke was a priest in the Church of England for twenty years, before leaving for fresh adventures. He worked for three years in a supermarket, stacking shelves and working on the till. He was also chair of the shop union. He has since left to go free lance, and now writes, leads retreats and offers consultancy.

He has written for *The Independent* and *The Evening Standard*, and is currently columnist with the *Daily Mail*. His weekly supermarket diary, 'Shelf Life', ran for 15 months in the *Mail on Saturday*, and he now contributes another weekly column called 'One-Minute Mystic.' The book version of *Shelf Life* has recently been published by Rider. The book version of *One-Minute Mystic* is published by Hay House in January 2010.

Other books by Simon include *Forsaking the Family* – a refreshingly real look at family life. Our families made us; yet we understand very little of how our experiences as children still affects us. The book starts by contemplating Jesus' ambivalence towards his own family, particularly his parents; reflects on how our family settings can both help and harm us; and suggests paths for freedom and authenticity.

The Beautiful Life – ten new commandments because life could be better was published by Bloomsbury, and describes ten skilful attitudes for life. Simon leads retreats around this book, and talks about it on this site. It is now also available in audio form with White Crow books.

Simon has been a teacher of the Enneagram for twenty years. The enneagram is an ancient and remarkable path of self-understanding, and Simon's book on the subject, published by Lion, is called *Enneagram – a private session with the world's greatest psychologist*.

Another bloody retreat is Simon's desert novel, describing events at the monastery of St James-the-Less set in the sands of Middle Egypt. It follows the fortunes of Abbot Peter and the rest of the community, when the stillness of their sacred setting is rudely and irrevocably shattered.

Simon was born in Sussex, but has lived and worked in London for twenty-five years. He has written comedy and satire for TV and radio, picking up a Sony radio award. He has two grown-up children and his hobbies include football, history and running. For more information, visit his website www.simonparke.com

Also available from White Crow Books

Marcus Aurelius—*The Meditations*
ISBN 978-1-907355-20-2

Elsa Barker—*Letters from
a Living Dead Man*
ISBN 978-1-907355-83-7

Elsa Barker—*War Letters
from the Living Dead Man*
ISBN 978-1-907355-85-1

Elsa Barker—*Last Letters
from the Living Dead Man*
ISBN 978-1-907355-87-5

Richard Maurice Bucke—
Cosmic Consciousness
ISBN 978-1-907355-10-3

G. K. Chesterton—*The
Everlasting Man*
ISBN 978-1-907355-03-5

G. K. Chesterton—*Heretics*
ISBN 978-1-907355-02-8

G. K. Chesterton—*Orthodoxy*
ISBN 978-1-907355-01-1

Arthur Conan Doyle—*The
Edge of the Unknown*
ISBN 978-1-907355-14-1

Arthur Conan Doyle—
The New Revelation
ISBN 978-1-907355-12-7

Arthur Conan Doyle—
The Vital Message
ISBN 978-1-907355-13-4

Arthur Conan Doyle with
Simon Parke—*Conversations
with Arthur Conan Doyle*
ISBN 978-1-907355-80-6

Leon Denis with Arthur Conan
Doyle—*The Mystery of Joan of Arc*
ISBN 978-1-907355-17-2

The Earl of Dunraven—*Experiences
in Spiritualism with D. D. Home*
ISBN 978-1-907355-93-6

Meister Eckhart with Simon
Parke—*Conversations
with Meister Eckhart*
ISBN 978-1-907355-18-9

Kahlil Gibran—*The Forerunner*
ISBN 978-1-907355-06-6

Kahlil Gibran—*The Madman*
ISBN 978-1-907355-05-9

Kahlil Gibran—*The Prophet*
ISBN 978-1-907355-04-2

Kahlil Gibran—*Sand and Foam*
ISBN 978-1-907355-07-3

Kahlil Gibran—*Jesus the Son of Man*
ISBN 978-1-907355-08-0

Kahlil Gibran—*Spiritual World*
ISBN 978-1-907355-09-7

Hermann Hesse—*Siddhartha*
ISBN 978-1-907355-31-8

D. D. Home—*Incidents
in my Life Part 1*
ISBN 978-1-907355-15-8

Mme. Dunglas Home; edited, with an Introduction, by Sir Arthur Conan Doyle—*D. D. Home: His Life and Mission*
ISBN 978-1-907355-16-5

Andrew Lang—*The Book of Dreams and Ghosts*
ISBN 978-1-907355-97-4

Edward C. Randall—*Frontiers of the Afterlife*
ISBN 978-1-907355-30-1

Lucius Annaeus Seneca—*On Benefits*
ISBN 978-1-907355-19-6

Rebecca Ruter Springer—*Intra Muros—My Dream of Heaven*
ISBN 978-1-907355-11-0

W. T. Stead—*After Death* or *Letters from Julia: A Personal Narrative*
ISBN 978-1-907355-89-9

Leo Tolstoy, edited by Simon Parke—*Tolstoy's Forbidden Words*
ISBN 978-1-907355-00-4

Leo Tolstoy—*A Confession*
ISBN 978-1-907355-24-0

Leo Tolstoy—*The Gospel in Brief*
ISBN 978-1-907355-22-6

Leo Tolstoy—*The Kingdom of God is Within You*
ISBN 978-1-907355-27-1

Leo Tolstoy—*My Religion: What I Believe*
ISBN 978-1-907355-23-3

Leo Tolstoy—*On Life*
ISBN 978-1-907355-91-2

Leo Tolstoy—*Twenty-three Tales*
ISBN 978-1-907355-29-5

Leo Tolstoy—*What is Religion and other writings*
ISBN 978-1-907355-28-8

Leo Tolstoy—*Work While Ye Have the Light*
ISBN 978-1-907355-26-4

Leo Tolstoy with Simon Parke—*Conversations with Tolstoy*
ISBN 978-1-907355-25-7

Howard Williams with an Introduction by Leo Tolstoy—*The Ethics of Diet: An Anthology of Vegetarian Thought*
ISBN 978-1-907355-21-9

All titles available as eBooks, and select titles available in Audiobook format from www.whitecrowbooks.com

Lightning Source UK Ltd.
Milton Keynes UK
174252UK00001B/27/P